TH

Ban

Gulf of

Map inside back cover.

The Vietnam War: Why?

The Vietnam War:

Why?

by M. Sivaram

CHARLES E. TUTTLE CO.
PUBLISHERS
Rutland, Vermont & Tokyo, Japan

Representatives
Continental Europe: BOXERBOOKS, INC., *Zurich*
British Isles: PRENTICE-HALL INTERNATIONAL, INC., *London*
Australasia: PAUL FLESCH & CO., PTY. LTD., *Melbourne*

Published by Charles E. Tuttle Co., Inc.
of Rutland, Vermont & Tokyo, Japan
with editorial offices at
Suido 1-chome, 2-6, Bunkyo-ku, Tokyo

© *1966 by Charles E. Tuttle Co., Inc.*
All rights reserved

Library of Congress
Catalog Card No. 66–11009

First edition, 1966
Fifth printing, 1966

Book design & typography
by Keiko Chiba

Printed in Japan

To

JANAMMA

whose love, faith and prayers
have sustained me in nearly thirty-five
years of adventures in journalism

Contents

Foreword

Assignment Vietnam is the newsman's nightmare. So much happens in that hapless land, and with such incredible speed, that he is unable to keep pace with the far-flung developments. In Vietnam, he is reporting a strange, baffling, frontless war—and an even stranger, more baffling, faceless political scene. They defy all ingenuity and powers of comprehension.

Millions of words have been written about Vietnam, and published and broadcast around the world. Yet Vietnam remains an enigma, the topic of worldwide controversy. After Korea and Suez, Malaya and Laos, and numerous other trouble spots of our time, I found Vietnam the most challenging beat in post-war journalism.

In a four-month assignment in Vietnam since early January, 1965, however, I enjoyed a privilege that seldom comes the way of newsmen. I had no harrassing deadline to meet, no temperamental editor to satisfy. I was able to watch the fast-shifting scenes on Vietnam's tangled military and political fronts with unhurried detachment.

The result is this modest volume. It does not add much to the current information on Vietnam. It does not attempt any deep analysis or assessment of the complex and confused situation in Vietnam. It is no more than a factual, objective straight-from-the-shoulder report on one of the most frustrating events in history, with its extremely grave implications for future developments in Asia.

Much of the material used in this book is based on personal study and observation. I have also drawn, liberally, from current literature on Vietnam and background studies made by several esteemed colleagues, Vietnamese editors and foreign correspondents. To them all, too many to be listed here, I express my gratitude for their contribution to an effort which, I hope, will help world understanding and appreciation of Vietnam.

I am also deeply grateful to the International Press Institute which posted me in Saigon at the most eventful period of the Vietnamese crisis and gave me not only an opportunity to refresh my acquaintance with the Vietnamese press in its own struggle for survival in the midst of a disastrous war, but also a ringside view of Southeast Asian history in the making.

M. Sivaram

Seoul, Republic of Korea

CHAPTER 1

Saigon, Oh, Saigon!

Saigon, you're so beautiful
Love and laughter so plentiful
Life's so gay, and so hectic
And the very air is so poetic
La la la la la la la . . .

THAT IS the Song of Saigon, one-time Paris of the East, for a long time a city virtually under Communist siege, and the world's number one trouble spot.

One night, after a hectic coup d'etat which made headlines throughout the world, I heard the young Vietnamese composer, Y. Van, sing his masterpiece on Saigon. The appeal was irresistible. Saigon is a fascinating city. Coups and counter-coups do not dampen its gaiety. Music and poetry pervade the air, even as the superjets pierce the sky with their deafening roar.

Saigon is an intriguing place, even apart from the complexities of the internal politics of South Vietnam and the unpredictable potentialities of a long-drawn-out war. It is a city of sharp contrasts and contradictions, that at once fascinate and baffle even the seasoned trouble-shooter.

Shortly before dusk, on a cool windy day in January, 1965, I was driving into Saigon from the Tan Son Nhut airport. It was the "crisis season" in Vietnam. The communist Vietcong were extraordinarily aggressive. They had just blown up an American military billet in the heart of the city. Saigon was just recovering from a partial coup and a major internal upheaval. And it was right in the midst of an agitation spearheaded by the Buddhists.

The tall young American, a research student, seated next to me in the airline bus, addressed me in excellent Hindi as we entered the crowded streets near the Air Vietnam offices. He was on his way home from India where he had spent nearly two years.

"Quite a strange and eerie place this. Don't you sense the air of tension around us?" he asked in all seriousness.

"Yes—and no," I replied tentatively, "we're in a war area and there has been plenty of trouble here lately."

There certainly was something unique about Saigon, something you could not see or feel, something that made you inexplicably uneasy.

The Tan Son Nhut airport was unlike other airports in Southeast Asia. It was littered with military aircraft and there were numerous people in uniform, Vietnamese as well as Americans. Military transport planes were landing and taking off frequently. Scores of skyraiders of the Vietnamese Air Force were huddled in one corner. Dozens of gleaming white American superjets crowded another corner. Helicopters were flying over the airport and the city all the time. And there were policemen carrying rifles.

Security precautions were strict. But it was all smiles and goodwill at the airport. Officials at the immigration post and customs were perhaps a little slow but extremely courteous and helpful. The formalities were elaborate but they went off smoothly. If there was a faint smell of tension, I had seen no other evidence of it.

My mind went back to the seventy sweltering minutes we spent inside the aircraft at the Pnom Penh airport, while the Air Vietnam plane from Bangkok deposited its cargo of tourists in Cambodia and took on those who had finished their sight-seeing in the country. Saigon-bound passengers were not allowed to land, while Cambodian security men stood guard at the door of the aircraft. It was a grueling halt. And, to reassure my young American friend, I remarked: "I thought Pnom Penh was more tense, though they didn't give us a chance to have a look at the place, even from the airport lounge!"

Tension or no tension, Saigon was far more hospitable. It has a charm, glamor and poise all its own, and a quaint capacity to make people feel at home, once they are there.

Saigon is a vast, sprawling city of tree-lined boulevards, towering skyscrapers, old colonial-style offices and residential houses, and new construction projects on all sides. Saigon is busy and booming, in spite of the war and the internal unrest, and to all appearances, it is a place of prosperity and plenty. Cholon, the adjoining Chinatown, is a beehive of trade and industry, with shops and stores displaying wide varieties of goods, innumerable hotels, bars and retaurants which are always crowded, and giant neon lights in fanciful designs that blaze throughout the night.

The corner table at the vast wide-open lounge of the old fashioned Hotel Continental Palace may not be the ideal observation post on Vietnamese affairs. But from that location, you can well get the 'feel' of Saigon and watch the entire city on parade before you. It looks out on the fabled Rue Catinat, now re-named Tu Do (Freedom) Street, and is right across from the modern Hotel Caravelle and the former Legislative Assembly, now Vietnam's House of Culture.

The colorful Saigon parade, as you watch it from the Hotel Continental lounge, begins at about eight o'clock in the morning and goes on until well past midnight, except during the afternoon siesta hours when the entire city goes to sleep between one and three o'clock.

Often big cars and station wagons, marked U.S. Army and U.S. Navy, slide past, crowding the bicycles and cyclos to the edge of the street, and almost every half an hour you hear the sirens wail, clearing the traffic for VIPs on their rounds.

Saigon is a city of bicycles, scooters, cyclos (trishas) and battered baby Renault taxis. Horns tooting, bells ringing, they rush helter-skelter and, if you are not used to the "keep to the right" traffic system, you get unnecessarily anxious about your safety. Saigon's taximen, however, will win any contest in rash driving, and accidents are frequent. Considering the way they go about, though, you are surprised there are not more mishaps.

Some of the big shops and department stores in downtown Saigon remind you of Tokyo and Singapore, though the goods on display are on a much smaller scale in variety and quantity. The markets are full, with rice, meat, poultry, fish, vegetables, fruits and flowers aplenty. Trade overflows into the sidewalks, displaying all sorts of consumer goods, curios and toys. Downtown Saigon is full of petty shops, run by young Vietnamese women, trim, erect and pretty in their high-collared "ao dais."

Girls in slim, gossamer gowns of pink and red, blue and yellow, gold and green, and every other color under the sun, lend an air of enchantment to the scenery before you. Occasionally, you find black-toothed Tongkinese women, with crowns of braided hair and drab "ao dais." These are refugees who came away from the communist north, though some of the wealthiest men and some of the most glamorous women in Saigon today are one-time refugees from communist rule.

By half past twelve in the afternoon, the streets of Saigon are deserted. Even the taxi driver refuses to stop. He, too, is off for his siesta. The old woman cigarette vendor suspends trade and curls up under her mobile shop. The cyclo driver pulls his cone-shaped palm leaf hat over his eyes and huddles himself in the passenger seat under the shadow of a tree.

French colonialism made its exit from Indochina, with Dien Bien Phu and the Geneva accords. But the rule of the siesta, introduced by the French colonial rulers, and the mandarins before them, still retains its grip on the people of Vietnam, including the communists under the Hanoi regime.

Saigon and its twin city of Cholon are really cities of the night. The main streets of both cities remind you of a miniature Ginza during the days of the American occupation in Tokyo. In a half square mile area in downtown Saigon, there are nearly two hundred bars and night clubs, catering mainly to the American troops and other foreigners. Each of these bars employs an average of twenty young Vietnamese girls. Flashy restaurants and shady establishments have sprung up all over the city and suburbs and they all seem to be doing excellent business, judging from the advertisements in the newspapers and the night-long rush of clients.

It is a sordid trade that goes on at most of the bars and night clubs of war-time Saigon. It is a quaintly vulgar type of trade in wine and women, with few parallels anywhere in the world. Vietnamese policemen keep silent vigil at the gates of the more notorious establishments, while respectable Vietnamese citizens, even those who resented Madame Ngo Dinh Nhu's call to puritanism, shun the sight of these symbols of social decadence, disfiguring the crusade against communism.

At almost any hour of the day or night you can see a hefty GI parading the streets, with a tiny Vietnamese girl hanging on to his arm. A small-time business man, carrying a file of Vietnamese paintings, accosts you at the street corner. With the common landscape paintings and prints he carries, he has other merchandise to offer—obscene photographs and masterpieces of pornography, if you happen to be interested in them. At the next crossing, the jaded old cyclo man invites you for a ride and whispers he will introduce you to "real number one." Other canvassers are louder and far more aggressive. They stop the pleasure-bound GI on his trek and shout: "Hey, Charlie, comear! Me have number one girl."

But there are GIs—and GIs; and you may watch the contrast from your observation post at the Continental lounge. There was one I knew, who was a lover of the waifs around the place. He used to take them in tow for a walk and buy them sweets and toys whenever he met them. Another was in the habit of carrying a little stray kid on his shoulders all around the House of Culture and leaving it on the square with whatever money he had on hand. Yet another GI used to have a lot of fun, buying up all the balloons from the vendor and distributing them among the street urchins.

The river bank in Saigon is a regular picnic spot. That is where the "ao dais" float in the wind, like a thousand multi-colored flags, and the city's middle class children gather for their evening out. The Saigon River is deep but comparatively narrow and the left bank is considered unsafe because of the Vietcong menace. All along the riverside walks, on the right bank, mobile restaurants ply their trade. Many sell Vietnamese food, with smoked fish that you can smell miles away. There are vendors of groundnuts, sugar-cane cones and a variety of delicious Vietnamese fruits. Next to the eating shops is a miniature park with a miniature golf course. At the edge of the river are numerous floating restaurants which cater mainly to the tourists. Up the river, just a few yards away, lies the Vietnamese naval squadron, all spic and span, ready to blaze away with the guns on the turret, while down river, not far off, is Saigon's modern port, with berthing facilities for the largest of ocean-going liners. Other big ships, lights blazing, flags fluttering in the wind, lie midstream in large numbers.

Saigon's hotels are always full. Residential accommodation is scarce and expensive. Even the slums are overcrowded. But life goes on normally, in spite of coups and crises, internal squabbles and external threats. Saigon is incredibly normal for a place that has not known normalcy for the best part of a quarter of a century.

The social whirl goes on, too, amidst political upheavals, bomb outrages and Vietcong terror. Jazz music from the bars vies with the slogan-shouting of the demonstrating mobs. Rotary Club dinners, women's association meetings, cultural functions, art exhibitions, go on according to schedule, even as the radio blares forth to announce the devastation caused by the latest American-Vietnamese air raids on targets in North Vietnam, or the casualty list in the big Vietcong bomb blast around the corner.

For a few brief minutes after the big bomb explosion that wrecked the United States Embassy in the heart of Saigon in March, 1965, killing sixteen and wounding well over a hundred people, the city seemed to be panic-stricken. But the recovery was quick. In less than half an hour, the lunch hour crowds were jostling and laughing on the sidewalks, a colorful wedding procession wended its way along busy Tu Do Street, and life in Saigon was again as gay and hectic as usual.

One evening I was at a cocktail party on the terrace of one of the tallest buildings on Saigon's main street. As the party warmed up, the host produced a tape-recorder and some of the guests started dancing to the jazziest of jazz. Amidst the wild music, the clinking of glasses and the loud good-humored chatter, a squadron of Skyraiders buzzed low over the city. Flares were seen being dropped at several locations in the suburbs, followed by the thunder of cannons all round. The party, however, went on merrily and nobody seemed to bother about the warlike operations above and around us.

At lunch time on February 19 I was at the Tan Son Nhut airport, to meet a friend who was passing through Saigon on his way from Bangkok to Manila. Suddenly, two Vietnamese Army tanks drove into the airport, one halting at the tarmac and the other rushing to the main runway, to enforce an order to close the airport to all traffic. Swiftly, the word went around that a military coup d'etat was on and that Saigon had fallen to the coup leaders. We sped out of the airport to the city, before someone else staged another lightning coup. On the way, we heard Radio Vietnam, which had been seized by the rebels, announce the take-over of the country. But in downtown Saigon, around Tu Do Street and Le Loi Avenue, it was all music and laughter and the cyclo men and painting peddlers were eagerly shouting "Hey, Charley!"

That night, somebody in authority clamped down the curfew at the unearthly hour of nine, crippling Saigon's major industry of wine, women and song. Everybody heaved a sigh of relief when the coup d'etat flopped the next morning and Saigon became its normal self again.

It is universally recognized that Saigon's bar life, its nightly entertainment activity, is very artificial and entirely commercial. The Vietnamese abhor it. The Americans are not in the least happy about it. Even the bar girls, hostesses and others engaged in the racket are not proud of it. But it is a flourishing trade.

Many of the bar girls and courtesans have come down from North Vietnam, where the Ho Chi Minh Government banned their trade, shaved the heads and knocked out the teeth of all offending females, and sent them to forced labor in concentration camps. The authorities in Saigon suspect that at least a small proportion of the bar women and playgirls may be in the pay of the communist Vietcong and the numerous protection gangs claiming to be agents of Vietcong terror and arson. But nobody in Vietnam has yet mustered enough courage to tamper with its music and laughter.

The late Ngo Dinh Diem, proud of his mandarin tradition, was disgusted with Saigon's gaiety, and shocked by its immorality. His sister-in-law, Madame Ngo Dinh Nhu, once ordered the closure of bars and night clubs. She outlawed dancing and threatened to clothe all women who did not conform to her standards of virtue in sack cloth. She scorned the American patrons of night clubs and dance halls. "If the Americans want to dance," she proclaimed, "they can dance with death."

There have been bomb outrages, and deaths, at Saigon's night spots frequented by Americans. Nevertheless, the show goes on. Anyone who tries to interfere with it will be promptly denounced as "number ten"—the most worthless character, in the new-fangled jargon of Saigon's play world.

Is Saigon indifferent to the crucial phase of the war going on around it? Have its people become so hardened to coups and crises that they just could not care less? Or is it a manifestation of the philosophy of making the best out of the time at your disposal; as a diversion from the unpleasant present and the uncertain future?

Even when France lay prostrate after Hitler's blitzkrieg,

and the Vichy Government lost its hold over Indochina, Saigon was a gay place. It was the same after tiny Thailand defeated the French colonial forces in Indochina in 1940–41 in a minor war along the frontiers, and annexed large areas of Cambodian and Laotian territory. With the advent of the Japanese before the outbreak of the Pacific War, French colonial prestige suffered heavily, but Saigon never abdicated its position as the Paris of the East. In fact, Japanese-occupied Saigon, with the French officials nominally in control, and the Vietnamese busy organizing resistance fronts, was still the most lively spot in war-time Southeast Asia.

The tradition continued in the post-war era, despite crises and conflicts. Saigon has remained almost changeless amidst the numerous changes of the twenty years since the end of the Pacific War. Vietnam has seen more strife and bloodshed than most nations in the region since the surrender of Japan. It has witnessed the exit of French colonialism, the partition of Vietnam, the upsurge of communism, the rise and fall of countless Governments, and a grim countrywide struggle which may escalate into a major war.

Fear and uncertainty have been Saigon's lot for more than twenty-five eventful years. These elements still dominate the outlook, but merging with them is a new faith that inspires the people of Saigon and all Vietnam. After the long ordeal, they seem confident that Saigon will never lose its gaiety, that Vietnam will never lose its freedom.

From the cluster of bars at the corner emerges a jubilant group, singing a merry tune:

Girlie, girlie, are you free,

For jolly GI on the spree?
Hey, hoi, beer, number one,
Ho Chi Meenh, number ten!

Taxis run about, canvassing last-minute clients before curfew hour. The old cyclo man, recovering from the effects of the pipe, yells "Hey, Charlie!" The street walker steps into a dim alley at the sight of the policeman on his beat.

But much of this crude gaiety is a transient show, in which the good people of Vietnam have no part. It is something that came in the wake of the internal and external strains to which their country has been exposed all these years.

Soon, the noise of dancing and music dies away. The neon lights fade. And Saigon regains its soul to the sweet chiming of bells from the glistening spire of the Buddhist temple and the imposing cathedral nearby. In the cool stillness of dawn, you watch Saigon in all its natural glory. Monks, chanting hymns, make it an occasion for solemnity. Burning joss sticks and incense fill the air with their fragrance.

But you seldom get a chance to contemplate for long the calm and splendor of dawn in Saigon. Suddenly, truckloads of troops, in jungle green, sporting rifles with fixed bayonets, rush past. You hear the rumbling of tanks in the distance. Helicopters fly about in swarms. Jet planes zoom across the sky. And you are back again at the nerve center of the bitter war in Vietnam.

CHAPTER 2

Blood, Sweat and Tears

A General can only be regarded as an authority on the art of attack, if his opponent does not know where he should defend himself. And, he is an authority on defense, only if his opponent does not know where he should attack.

Sun Tsue Wu

THE CITY OF SAIGON, in its strange sophistication and stranger lapses into cynicism, is seldom in tune with the Vietnamese countryside. It is there, in the jungles and mountains, the little hamlets astride the green paddy-fields, and the fishing villages along the lengthy coastline, that the dance with death goes on, almost non-stop, in a dirty, ruthless, wandering war, which has no visible front lines. And the men who wage this incredible war are keen disciples of old General Sun Tsue Wu, the Chinese strategist and father of guerilla warfare, who lived sometime in the fifth century B.C.

Communist China's Mao Tze-tung and his trusted lieutenant Chu Teh translated the ancient general's theory into action in the so-called "People's War" to seize power from the Chiang Kai-shek regime. Mao Tze-tung's thesis on "liberation" wars represents an exact copy of Sun Tsue Wu's dictum: "Rouse the enemy, should he remain quiet. Make him march when he pitches camp. And always appear when the opponent must follow you in order to defend himself. March swiftly in, where the enemy does not expect you."

It is Mao Tze-tung who is the author of the basic blueprint for the long weary war in Vietnam. The man who has translated it into Vietnamese terms is the hero of Dien Bien Phu, North Vietnam's Defense Minister, General Vo Nguyen Giap. He has analyzed guerilla war as a protracted conflict, progressing through three stages —concealed mobilization and guerilla forays; larger but still highly mobile operations; and, finally, the classic conventional military offensive.

Giap's dictum: "Only a long-term war enables us to transform our weakness into strength. Thousands of small victories accumulate a great success."

This has been the basic pattern of the war in Vietnam. The first phase of concealed mobilization and hit-and-run raids by guerilla bands is over. The second phase of larger mobile operations has been highly successful in many areas of South Vietnam. Giap's Vietcong have accumulated thousands of small victories. The year 1965 was probably designated as the beginning of the classic, conventional, large scale offensive. The preliminary campaign of terror and subversion rocked the city of Saigon and the major towns. Regular battalions of the North Vietnamese Army took up positions south of the 17th parallel. Large shipments of arms, ammunition and supplies started moving down to Vietcong camps along the coastline and in the mountain hideouts. The Vietcong agents seemed seized with kamikaze (suicide squad) fervor. In daring raids, they began blowing up American bases in Danang, Pleiku and other centers south of the parallel.

Then, suddenly, the outlook changed. The South Vietnamese and their American allies decided that, if the North Vietnamese armed forces and guerillas could cross the border, it was well within their own rights to cross the frontier to the north by air, if not by land. A "new look" war emerged, with the South Vietnamese and American aircraft blasting North Vietnamese military installations and communication lines, necessitating drastic changes in General Giap's blueprint.

But the grim conflict grinds on, in all its savagery, across the tortured land. The daily war communique, issued by the Saigon Government, lists scores of operations, large and small, in almost every part of the country. Average Vietcong casualties, on a normal day, are about a hundred; casualties on the Government side number about half. The Government Communique lists a series of raids, ambushes, "search and destroy" missions, seizures of arms and ammunition dumps and a variety of other military operations, including an occasional "pitched battle." It has been a tale of blood and steel, sweat and tears, for millions of Vietnamese for the best part of two decades.

South of Saigon, in the fertile Mekong delta, live nearly eight million Vietnamese, mostly small-time peasants. Their's is a sweltering world, a world of luscious green and bright yellow by day, a world of darkness and fear by night. The entire delta area is flat, with the exception of two little hills which rise incongruously above the vast stretches of paddyfields. The French had built watch-towers along the roads and the Vietnamese, with American aid, have rebuilt them, at intervals of nearly a kilometer.

High above the military convoys on the roads, the buffaloes in the fields, the bare-bodied men at the plough, and the clusters of peasant huts along the winding streams, sentries keep watch for Vietcong bands. The Vietcong follow the guerilla textbook in every detail. They move about quietly, secretly, often seeking and secur-ing the protection of the villagers. And the sentry usually wakes up only when it is too late. Frequently the Vietcong stage hit-and-run attacks and retreat to their hideouts in the face of gunfire from the security forces.

There are two rival administrations in most parts of the Mekong Delta—the legal government with its head-quarters in Saigon, and the illegal government operated by the communists. One may drive out of Saigon for ten or fifteen miles—by daylight only. Beyond that, nobody is safe at any time. The Vietcong operate mobile check points and hold up traffic on any of the main roads or on the village tracks. The Saigon Government's writ does not go very far from the capital, in spite of its military strength and the concerted anti-Vietcong operations of the past several years.

The lights go out at dusk at most of the hamlets in the Mekong delta. Then, the people await the Vietcong attack. Fear stalks the villages. But the people do fight back. They know what to do, and where to go, in the event of an attack by the Vietcong guerillas. They have their self-defense corps. But they can never guess the strength of the attacking Vietcong bands or the type of attack they mount. It is the Vietcong, not the Vietnamese villagers, who are adept at the tactics of strategist Sun Tsue Wu and his modern disciples in Peking and Hanoi.

A few years ago, during the late Ngo Dinh Diem regime, the South Vietnamese, alarmed by the Vietcong advances in the Mekong delta, started building "strategic hamlets" on the pattern set by the British authorities during the days of the anti-communist emergency in Malaya. The plan aimed at providing security for the villagers on the one hand, and depriving the communists of the support and protection of the rural folk on the other. In Malaya, the project worked well, and helped isolate the rebels from the people. Eventually, the rebels were either starved out of existence or forced to come out and fight in the open.

In Vietnam, however, the strategic hamlets program failed to produce the desired results. Ngo Dinh Nhu, the brother of former President Diem who was in charge of Vietnam's internal security, went into the mass production of strategic villages. Without warning, preparation or consent, hundreds of thousands of Vietnamese peasants in the Mekong delta and elsewhere saw their homes and their belongings burned behind them. They were uprooted at bayonet point and ordered to settle down in Nhu's ready-made strategic hamlets, far away from their own localities, which meant that they lost not only their homes but also their land.

The Malayan pattern was different. There, they started

building strategic hamlets in the non-communist areas, and worked out through the disputed zones into the communist-dominated areas. Mr. Nhu, in his enthusiasm, and with the enormous power he wielded, did not stop to make the hamlets worthy of popular support.

Nevertheless, the idea of strategic hamlets to cope with the Vietcong insurgents seemed to work for some time. Small teams of American instructors went into the hamlets to teach the people how to fight the Vietcong intruders. They helped the build-up of defenses around their areas and slept with guns and grenades by their side. They became marked men. The Vietcong attacks increased. Casualties mounted, among them hundreds of village chiefs and resistance leaders. Many villages soon became strategic strongholds of Vietcong agents. Mr. Nhu's "operation sunrise" became "operation sunset." The countryside echoed to the din of continuous war.

By early 1965, large areas of the rolling Mekong delta, Vietnam's rice bowl, were over-run by the Vietcong. There were large-scale attacks on the big air base in Noctrang, near the tip of the Peninsula, and a number of important military installations in the region, indicating a significant change in the take-over tactics. Even the well-guarded holiday resorts on the coast, famed for their sandy beaches and swaying palms, became unsafe after dusk.

The Annamite mountain chain, running parallel to the east coast of the Indochina Peninsula, is similar to the Western Ghats, on India's Arabian Sea coastline. East of the mountain ranges lies the desolate hinterland of Laos. South of it is the state of Cambodia. Vast numbers of the Vietcong from the north have come into South Vietnam through the Ho Chi Minh trail in Laos, while Cambodia, hostile to the Saigon regime, has been an easy sanctuary, albeit a temporary one, for the Vietcong and other elements plaguing South Vietnam.

This part of Vietnam is as varied in its terrain and population as it is pretty and picturesque in its natural beauty. The central Vietnam highlands are inhabited by various tribes. They grow rubber, coffee, tea, timber and various other cash crops. The hill tribes, though highly sophisticated, are still known as "montagnards." They resisted the Vietcong terror and reduced the communist influence in the region to negligible proportions. Work on the plantations goes on fairly smoothly. But this, according to Saigon gossip, is because the planters, mainly Frenchmen, have come to a working appeasement deal with the Vietcong agents.

Almost the entire lowlands astride the mountain ranges are under Vietcong influence, in varying degrees. The thriving little towns and the thickly populated fishing centers along the coast, with miles and miles of paddyland and coconut plantations, are all heavily infiltrated by the Vietcong. It is there that the Vietcong suicide squads have been in action against the American military installations. This region has also been the delivery point for the bulk of arms and ammunition from Hanoi and other communist capitals, to bolster the Vietcong insurrection south of the 17th parallel.

Just below the dividing line and the demilitarized zone is the land of the Perfumed River and the Mandarin Road around Hue, which was once the seat of the Emperors of Annam. The River of Perfumes still flows through the ancient town, but it is crowded with junks and clusters of water hyacinth and water lily. The pungent aroma of cinnamon plantations still commands your attention, but the smell of war fumes all around is inescapable.

Wartime Hue is a booming town and a major attraction for holiday-makers, but it has lost much of its ancient charm and glory. Traditional princely homes have become dilapidated. Near them, new concrete structures have risen in large numbers. The age-old marble mountain stands mute, near the Da Nang air base. It is from this vast air center on the east coast of central Vietnam that scores of American jets take off almost daily to blast the communist military installations in North Vietnam. The roar of the jets and of the swarms of helicopters over this vital township fills the air for miles around. But here, too, as in the lowlands in the south, the Vietcong roam about almost at will. Helicopters and Skyraiders stage surprise attacks, raiding parties smash up Vietcong camps and staging bases, but the campaign goes on, without the slightest let-up.

Vietcong guerillas blew up the American residential quarters at the Da Nang air base and an equally important military station at Pleiku, leading to the series of reprisal raids on North Vietnam in February and the landing of United States marine battalions to bolster the security of the American bases. But the Vietcong still carry on with their deadly assaults.

It is in this region that the Vietcong may first launch the third phase of General Giap's take-over strategy with conventional warfare, deploying large forces. A few battalions of the regular North Vietnamese Army were already massing for this grand finale when the "new look" war emerged on Vietnam, with the South Vietnamese and the Americans capturing the initiative, destroying the staging bases and supply lines of the communist North Vietnamese regime.

The Vietcong guerillas and their patrons in Hanoi claim that they have "liberated" almost three-quarters of South Vietnam, with control over more than fifty percent of the country's inhabitants. This is an exaggerated claim but there is no doubt that the communist forces, operating in South Vietnam, have fulfilled General Giap's target of a thousand small victories, accumulating to a big success. The South Vietnamese authorities claim that their security forces have killed at least 75,000 Vietcong and captured 14,000 since 1960. Over the same period of five years, the Vietcong ranks, in active operation in South Vietnam, rose from a few thousand fanatics to nearly 80,000 regular troops and more than 100,000 guerillas.

The South Vietnamese armed forces have been growing in strength but they are still inadequate to deal with the vast "ghost army" of communists in the countryside. In spite of almost U.S. $3.5 billion in aid to South Vietnam over the last ten years and the supply of tanks, artillery, aircraft, chemical defoliants and well over 60,000 American military and civilian personnel to assist and advise the South Vietnamese, the Vietcong threat has remained as acute as ever. For all their military superiority, the South Vietnamese and their American advisers have been unable to find an effective answer to old-time strategist Sun Tsue Wu and his modern counterparts in Peking and Hanoi.

In six years, the Vietcong have assassinated 13,000 village headmen in the territory of South Vietnam. They have impressed thousands of villagers as laborers and camp followers. They have been collecting "taxes" from peasants, passengers on buses and bicycles. They have been raiding police posts, kidnapping officials, and just mowing down people who refused to take orders from them.

They combine with this campaign of terrorism and murder the usual communist propaganda pledges, spicing them with lively accounts of the political instability and corruption in Saigon and the alleged domination of South Vietnam by the American imperialists. The Vietnamese villager, imbued with considerable common sense, seldom accepts the communist propaganda line, but his instinct for self-preservation often makes him a reluctant victim of Vietcong treachery and tyranny. He is ready to fight for his "liberation" but the Government in Saigon has been way behind the peasant in the countryside in this crucial war.

In spite of the vagaries on South Vietnam's political front, and the squabble within the top leadership of the armed forces, the Vietnamese army, trained and advised by the cream of the American military services, has been waging a heroic campaign against the Vietcong. But it has to cope with an enemy that is as resourceful as it is deadly.

The Vietcong bands are masters of concealment, camouflage and treachery. With green leaves and twigs thrust into the net that covers his basketwork helmet and the pack on his back, the Vietcong soldier blends himself into the roadside foliage at the sound of an aircraft. He stays for hours in a pond, or in a flooded paddyfield, with a bamboo breathing tube.

Without favorable odds, the Vietcong just will not fight. They are past-masters in the art of ambush. Often, they overrun a small outpost, then lie in wait for the government column expected to relieve the post. The Vietcong's network of spies promptly informs them of the route of the relief column. They mine the routes of entry and retreat and dig in alongside for their prey. This is a trick that has worked time and again and the government forces have yet to devise the counter-strategy.

Since the beginning of 1965, the Vietcong have streamlined their organization and operational methods. They have evolved a set-up almost parallel to that maintained by the Saigon Government. On the first rung of the structure are units of the popular force militia, part-time guerillas who till the fields by day and fight at night. The district forces, above the part-time soldiers, are better armed and trained and are full-time guerillas and card-carrying members of the communist party. But they fight only within their own respective provinces. At the top are the hard core "liberation" forces in uniform, and equipped with modern arms produced in communist bloc countries or captured American weapons. Man to man, these Vietcong soldiers are superior to the Government forces. It is the air cover, which the Government forces usually call into play, that tilts the scale in their favor in all routine operations against the Vietcong.

But airpower, abundantly at the disposal of the anti-communist forces, is at once a blessing and a curse in the unique warfare in Vietnam. The daily war communiques

list scores of air operations within South Vietnam, against
Vietcong camps, assault areas, arms dumps and hideouts.
But air attacks hurt people on the sidelines, too, and that
provides useful grist for communist propaganda against
the Saigon Government and the Americans, and in pre-
judicing the villagers against them. The advantage of
aerial superiority is undoubtedly substantial in a conventional war. In tracking down the shadows in the thickets
of the Vietnamese jungle however, it has serious limitations. It cannot bring about a decisive victory, and it
hurts innocent bystanders.

In the remote areas of rural Vietnam, the peasant in
the paddyfield squats on the ground and stays still and
silent at the sight of a helicopter. The slightest movement
by him might arouse the suspicion of the pilot of the low-
flying copter. The pilot is never sure whether the man on
the ground is a Vietcong or an innocent peasant and he
may be tempted to open fire in self-defense. If anything
like that happens, the Government loses the sympathy and
support of the entire village. Air operations are fraught
with various types of dangers in the peculiar warfare in
Vietnam.

But the mortal struggle continues unabated. The Vietcong campaign of kidnap and murder knows no bounds.
Last February, an American officer drove just six miles
out of Saigon and the Vietcong grabbed him with ease.
He has not been heard of since. A British businessman, on
a boat ride in the Saigon river, was whisked away by the
Vietcong just two miles down the busy harbor. He was
released after weeks of hush-hush negotiations and there

have been wild guesses regarding the terms of the deal with the Vietcong.

The city of Saigon, with all its gaiety, is a prison without walls. And so are the major towns of South Vietnam, caught in a war without front lines, against an invisible but deadly enemy.

"The highest perfection of warfare," wrote General Sun Tsue Wu for the benefit of Mao, Giap and other disciples, "is to be able to break the opponent's resistance without too much effort and to capture the enemy's territory undamaged."

The Vietcong got quite close to the grand goal early in 1965. Since then, however, the target has been as elusive as their ghost army in the jungles and mountains.

Today, the Vietcong and their patrons in Hanoi and Peking have two alternatives before them. They must either risk a full-scale open war, which will not be another Dien Bien Phu for Giap and his hordes. Or, they must get set for a tactical retreat and revise the time-honored textbook on guerilla warfare.

CHAPTER 3

The Faceless War

The major victories of the liberation army have created conditions for guerilla warfare to develop further and more rapidly, to deal thunder blows at the enemy.

—*Lao Dong party's proclamation*

WHAT IS this conflict in Vietnam? Is it a civil war within the Republic of Vietnam? Or is it a war of resistance against unprovoked aggression? Is it a conflict in which the people of South Vietnam have risen up in arms to overthrow an unpopular government? Or are the South Vietnamese Government and people engaged in a desperate struggle against armed forces which have crossed internationally-recognized frontiers to invade and occupy large areas of their country?

The issue is being debated around the world. Pious advocates of peace and academically-inclined politicians often raise the subject in the context of the danger of a larger conflagration arising from the war in Vietnam. But attempts to twist facts, or ignore realities, can never serve the cause of peace. For the war in Vietnam is a war of resistance against armed aggression. And the world has it on the authority of North Vietnam's President Ho Chi Minh!

For more than twenty years, Ho Chi Minh's soldiers and communist party cadres have operated in Vietnam, north and south, under various names. In 1941, Ho Chi Minh's political organization was known as the Vietnam Loc Lap Dong Minh (Vietnam Independence Organization). It went through various transformations in the course of the long struggle against the Japanese and the French. The Democratic Party, the Radical Socialist Party, the People's Revolutionary Party and many other organizations were merely different names for Ho Chi Minh's communist party at different phases of the communist conquest of Vietnam. Today, in North Vietnam, the communists have no more use for any mask for the deception of the masses. The Hanoi regime is the rule of the Lao Dong (Communist) Party. And the so-called National Front for the Liberation of South Vietnam, under whose flag the communist Vietcong are supposed to be operating, is a creation of Ho Chi Minh's Lao Dong Party with its headquarters in Hanoi.

The first announcement of the formation of the South Vietnam "liberation front" came in February 1961—from Hanoi. This followed a policy decision of the Lao Dong (Communist) Party of North Vietnam, in its plot to lend an air of legitimacy to the North Vietnamese campaign of subversion and terror in the south. A resolution of Ho Chi Minh's Lao Dong Party said that "the major victories of the Vietcong had created conditions for guerilla warfare to develop further and more rapidly, to deal thunder blows at the enemy."

The North Vietnam communists set up the organization as a propaganda vehicle and as a means of camouflaging their hostilities as a legitimate liberation movement. To them, it was a strategic necessity following the decision to conquer South Vietnam by force of arms. The Liberation Front's manifesto, drafted and approved in Hanoi, perfected the illusion. It claimed that the Front's urgent task was the overthrow of the Saigon Government and the establishment of "a broad national democratic coalition administration" in South Vietnam. Thereafter, the manifesto said, the Front would "negotiate the unification of North and South Vietnam and pursue a foreign policy based on peace and neutrality." In the domestic sphere, the Front promised "democracy and social justice, full employment and land reforms."

In Vietnamese there is a word for ghosts, phantoms, demons and other non-existent things. It is "ma." And Ho Chi Minh's liberation Front is the most frightening "ma" that haunts the people of South Vietnam.

The communists have endowed the so-called liberation front with all the trappings of a popular movement. A former Saigon lawyer named Nguyen Huu Tho is proclaimed to be the leader of the Front. It claims to have a Central Committee of fifty members who, according to Hanoi Radio broadcasts, include "persons from far and near, from the 17th parallel to the tip of the Camau peninsula, from the coastal plains, the delta, the jungle and frontier, from the rural areas and temporarily occupied cities, from all social classes, nationalities, religions, political, cultural and professional tendencies."

Propaganda is the organization's principal mission, and the South Vietnam Liberation Front has secured a certain amount of public attention in countries aligned with the Communists. Foreign communist party recognition and support are used by Hanoi as a magnifying mirror designed to reflect the front's legitimacy and importance. The Front sends performing troupes to communist gatherings, and has set up "diplomatic missions" in Prague, Algiers, East Berlin and Cuba.

It is on the home front that the so-called Liberation Front has found it difficult to establish its credibility. The communists are hated by the people of South Vietnam, even those who are disgusted with the long-drawn-out war and the suffering and privation it has meant. Everybody knows that the men who have lent their names to the Liberation Front are agents, dupes and victims of the Communist regime in Hanoi and slaves of the Vietcong terrorists engaged in the campaign of sabotage and murder.

The new tempo of the war, and the fear of a major flare-up which may not turn out to be in their favor, have demoralized the Front's leadership. With the Hanoi regime's inability to cope with the mounting air assaults and Peking's reluctance to get involved in the Vietnam conflict, the Liberation Front leaders are highly embarrassed in the role they have assumed. All they can do is to go on singing their masters' tune; otherwise, they run the risk of being liquidated by the Vietcong who are supposed to form the military wing of their movement.

Just as the Mao-Giap textbook on guerilla warfare hit the snag in the South Vietnamese theater of operations, the classic communist propaganda tactics have proved ineffective in South Vietnam. The creation of the Liberation Front was aimed at perpetrating a fraud on the people of South Vietnam and the world. It implied that there was an alien or unpopular government in South Vietnam and that the good patriots of the land had banded together to liberate the country. The pretension was that it was, indeed, a revolt within South Vietnam against the government in Saigon which, it was alleged, was dominated by the United States.

The plain fact, however, is that the Government in Saigon, whatever its limitations, has always been more independent of American influence than the government in Hanoi has been of the dictates of Peking and Moscow. The Saigon government, with all its drawbacks, is more representative of the people in South Vietnam than the Hanoi Government has ever been representative of the people in North Vietnam. When Saigon charges Hanoi with aggression, it is undisputed fact. The bulk of the Vietcong troops and guerilla bands are from North Vietnam. It is Hanoi that directs and controls their operations. The so-called South Vietnam Liberation Front is an agency of the Lao Dong (Communist) Party of North Vietnam.

ʾThe seeds of the Vietcong war were sewn even before the ink was dry on the 1954 Geneva agreement that ended French colonialism in Indochina. The Geneva accord climaxed nine years of warfare between the French forces and the Viet Minh, the anti-French nationalist elements which sought to overthrow the colonial regime. What is now communist North Vietnam was the scene of bitter battles between the French and Viet Minh forces. The final rout of the French came with the epic battle of Dien Bien Phu, in which Ho Chi Minh's movement, then known as the Vietnam Independence Organization, crushed the French colonial army of nearly a quarter million officers and men.

Under the Geneva agreement, Indochina was divided into four independent states—Cambodia, Laos and North and South Vietnam. Since then, Ho Chi Minh and his army commander, General Giap, the hero of Dien Bien Phu, have been planning and campaigning for the annexation of South Vietnam, the establishment of Laos as a communist satellite and the eventual take-over of Cambodia to complete communist domination of all Indochina.

After the Geneva agreement, nearly a million people from North Vietnam came down to non-communist South Vietnam. About a tenth of that number, who presumably preferred communist rule, migrated northward. In 1954, there were probably a couple of thousand armed Vietcong from the north, operating in the jungles and mountains of South Vietnam. The influx of refugees, escaping the tyranny of the communist regime in the north, went on for some time. With these refugees, and in other isolated groups, came large numbers of well-armed and heavily indoctrinated communists to carry out political propaganda and subversion, as well as hit-and-run raids on villages and security posts. This campaign of harassment went on interminably but the Saigon Government was preoccupied with other and more pressing problems.

It was estimated that in 1958, four years after the Geneva agreement, there were not more than 5,000 armed Vietcong guerillas from the north active in South Vietnam. Many of these were men who, under instructions from Ho Chi Minh, stayed on in the South, pretending to resume civilian life while waiting for the call to action.

In the first flush of victory at Dien Bien Phu, Ho Chi Minh had hoped to capture South Vietnam without a fight. That is probably why he agreed to the partition. The Geneva agreement had called for elections to establish a single government for all Vietnam in 1956. Ho Chi Minh's record as the hero of Vietnam's freedom struggle and his iron grip over the fifteen million people in the north, assured him an easy victory over any candidate emerging from among the fourteen million Vietnamese in the South, riddled by political differences and internal unrest. Probably sensing this danger, South Vietnam's late President Ngo Dinh Diem refused to hold the elections, on the plea that the Saigon Government was not a signatory to the Geneva agreement and was not, therefore, bound by its terms.

The result was that Ho Chi Minh called out his underground army and launched the reign of terror in South Vietnam, strengthening the campaign with a steady flow of trained troops and sabotage gangs from the north. By 1960 the war had gained tremendous momentum, and Ho set up the South Vietnam Liberation Front, while Giap accelerated the guerilla warfare program, and set about making preparations for invasion.

It is a vast, well-armed North Vietnamese armed force that now goes by the name of Vietcong. From infiltration and subversion, night raids and assassinations, the invaders have turned to mobile warfare, using as many as two thousand men in a single operation, against the maximum of a hundred a couple of years ago. The invading forces come in by land and sea, by junks along the coastline and by jungle tracks through Laotian territory. In February, the South Vietnamese captured a shipload of arms and ammunition off the east coast. There was enough to equip an entire army division, it had been manufactured in communist China, Soviet Russia, Czechoslovakia and other countries. It was shipped directly from the North Vietnamese port of Haiphong. This big arms seizure coincided with the Vietcong's change of tactics to mobile warfare and pitched battles.

The campaign, which has become increasingly intense and widespread since 1963, amounts to deliberate aggression, a diabolic communist bid to conquer the State of South Vietnam. At the Geneva conference, both North and South Vietnam were represented, but only the Hanoi regime signed the agreement. Officially, the South refused to accept the Geneva decisions, though recognizing that it had no means of resisting them. The South was against partition, while the North accepted partition because it had no intention whatever of abiding by its terms.

With more than a million refugees pouring into the South from the North, after the Geneva pact, the South had a vast potential fifth-column to create disturbances in the North, if the Saigon government had decided to embark on such a move. But the Ngo Dinh Diem regime, busy with the pacification of the country and consolidating the family's hold on the regime, adhered to the Geneva accord. Besides, Saigon did not wish to come in conflict with the International Control Commission, comprising India, Canada and Poland, created under the Geneva agreement to keep the peace in divided Vietnam.

The official position of the South Vietnamese government was that it did not recognize the Commission and its activities, but it welcomed the Commission, extended all the necessary facilities for its work and adhered to the Geneva commitments. North Vietnam, however, evolved its own code of conduct in dealing with the International Control Commission. The Hanoi authorities ordered the closure of airports when military supplies—prohibited under the Geneva agreement—were being landed, and the ICC was politely asked to stay home. Important military checkposts were closed to ICC inspection, whenever the commission's presence did not suit communist activities.

The Commission, by the very nature of its composition and the absence of any real authority, was never able to function as an effective peace-keeping body. It received complaints of Geneva Pact violations from both sides, but was unable to do anything tangible about them. While South Vietnam has invariably substantiated the complaints by it and assisted the Commission to verify them, the Northern regime merely wanted the complaints to go on record, without verification by the Commission.

A classic example was the Hanoi complaint against the bombing of fishing villages on Tiger Island, off the Vietnamese coast, in February, 1965. Although it is true the island was bombed by the South Vietnamese Air Force, the targets were not fishing villages but naval installations and radar stations. When the Commission suggested that its members be allowed to make an on-the-spot check, the North Vietnam Government advanced the plea that it was unable to guarantee their safety.

It is on this security plea to cover up military movements that Hanoi has immobilized the International Commission following the South Vietnamese-American air raids. The ICC teams were asked to quit all check posts in North Vietnam. When the Commission members suggested that such an order should come from the Geneva co-chairmen, the Hanoi authorities insisted on enforcing their demand and, in one or two cases, threatened to cut off food and water supply to the ICC villas. In at least one case, ICC men were bundled into cars brought by so-called liaison officers, and whisked off to Hanoi.

The Geneva co-chairmen remain, but the chair seems vacant and the agreement they evolved is non-existent. The ICC men are still in Vietnam, dutifully recording and transmitting charges of violation of the Geneva agreements, hoping and praying for an early end of the thankless assignment. The Hanoi regime has openly announced that it has no more use for the ICC. The Saigon government presumably believes that the ICC should be able to produce ample evidence of North Vietnam aggression if the issue is raised at any international conference.

It is meaningless to recall the Geneva agreement and advocate a return to it under the existing realities in Vietnam. The Hanoi regime never intended to adhere to the Geneva accord, which it began violating even before it was signed. Recent actions of the Saigon government and armed forces may constitute a violation of the Geneva agreement, but there is a major difference in the way the two sides in Vietnam have treated the pact.

South Vietnam's actions have been open and above-board. It has made no treacherous pretensions, and whatever it has done has been in self-defense and retaliation against the aggressive campaign launched, directed and controlled by Hanoi. American aid, which has been pouring into South Vietnam, has been widely advertised. The U.S. aid program in the defense of South Vietnam is no secret. The developments in the South, regardless of whether or not they constitute a technical violation of the Geneva agreement, have been well known to the ICC and the world at large.

The drawbacks of the South Vietnamese government are many but, again, there has been no attempt to conceal them or to minimize them. Under the none-too-perfect system of democracy that operates in South Vietnam, the people enjoy some right to express their dissatisfaction with government policies and the conduct of the men in power. The government in Hanoi, which operates on the totalitarian system, may pretend that it is a popular regime, but in fact it is a tyranny based on the Peking model. The only known revolt against the autocracy in Hanoi flared up in Ho Chi Minh's home province of Nyge An, following the hideous brutalities of the communist land reform program in 1956. If there have been other internal upheavals, the world has not heard much of them from the police state that is North Vietnam.

It would have been possible for the South to instigate a revolt in the North but, in a society under communist control, it would have been a formidable task. On the other hand, it was relatively easy for the North Vietnam communists to infiltrate in force into South Vietnam, with political propaganda and subversion at the beginning, and finally moving to open warfare.

In 1947, immediately after the partition of the Indian sub-continent, Pakistan sent tribal raiders into the Indian State of Kashmir, followed by regular units of the Pakistani army. The war was stopped before it spread and the ceasefire line, under U.N. supervision, is still respected by both sides after eighteen years, though there have been occasional incidents and the dispute itself still remains unsettled. Fortunately, the cold war element did not get beyond the surface in the Kashmir dispute. The latest clash, in the region of the Rann of Kutch, in western India, however, may have far more serious repercussions because, to all indications, Communist China might well be the power behind the latest spate of aggression.

If, instead of the limited aggression in Kashmir, Pakistan had launched a large scale and deliberate campaign of taking over India, by first sending in guerilla bands and then the regular armed forces, and if the insidious plot engulfed the entire country, the situation would be very much similar to that pervading in South Vietnam. It is futile to designate aggression by any other name. There is absolutely no evidence that the Vietcong has any significant popular following in South Vietnam. And the acceptance of aggression, however expedient it might seem, will only increase the aggressor's appetite.

The communist attempt to conquer non-communist

Korea in 1950 was essentially similar to the communist war in Vietnam. The methods, however, were different in Korea, where they tried to stage a big military sweep down the peninsula. North Korea's Kim Il-Sung's Moscow-oriented tactics encountered unexpected resistance and even Communist China's entry into the war did not result in victory for the aggressors.

Ho Chi Minh resorted to deeper and more subtle methods in South Vietnam, but it should not confuse the basic issue or camouflage the objectives of the campaign. If Kim Il-Sung and Communist China were guilty of aggression in Korea, Ho Chi Minh and his patrons in Peking are equally guilty of aggression in Vietnam. Communist China has been hesitant about taking the plunge in Vietnam but it has refused to use its power to call off the war of aggression.

Perhaps the forces of aggression in Southeast Asia have concluded a secret pact of their own.

Indonesia's President Sukarno has apparently learned his anti-Malaysia "confrontation" tactics from Uncle Ho in Hanoi and his allies in Peking. When Sukarno talks of long-term confrontation, with guerilla warfare and the landing of "invasion" parties by sea and air, with the attendant campaign of sabotage and subversion in Malaysia, he probably hopes to achieve what Ho Chi Minh has achieved in South Vietnam in the last few years.

Unlike South Vietnam, Malaysia is endowed with national unity, patriotic leadership and a stable administration and has the benefit of its defense pact with Britain. But if Sukarno's undeclared war constitutes aggression against Malaysia, Ho Chi Minh's war in South Vietnam cannot belong to a different category of human behavior.

Significantly, in both these faceless, frontless wars, the strings are pulled from Peking and the performance follows the Sun Tsue Wu script, revised by Mao Tze-tung. And if Sukarno and the Indonesian Communist Party play the title role in the confrontation drama against Malaysia, Mao has assigned the same role to Ho Chi Minh and the Lao Dong party of North Vietnam.

CHAPTER 4

A Nation in Travail

Change is constant; and the question is, not whether you should resist change which is inevitable, but whether that change should be carried out in deference to the manners, the customs, the laws and the traditions of the people.

Disraeli

THE YEAR of the Dragon was amazingly eventful for Vietnam. And, when it finally lapsed into history at the end of January 1965, it left behind a trail of floods and typhoons, coups and counter-coups, confusion and chaos, and the threat of a communist take-over of the country.

Vietnamese elders and astrologers believed that 1965, the Year of the Snake, heralded a far more auspicious period for the embattled nation. It may be difficult to strike a reconciliation between the allegedly noble attributes of the snake, which guided the destiny of the country during 1965, and the ignoble portents on the war front and the uncertainties in the political sphere. But astrological forecasts of "refreshing trends" in the national outlook by April at least seem to have been unexpectedly accurate.

Two days before the dawn of the Year of the Snake, South Vietnam's Chief of State, Phan Khac Suu, was having an informal chat with two leading journalists. The atmosphere in the capital was tense. A Buddhist agitation for the dismissal of the government headed by Premier Tran Van Houng had hit the climax of intensity. Five leading Buddhist dignitaries had gone on a "fast unto death." The Buddhists believed that the United States Embassy and Ambassador Maxwell Taylor were supporting Houng and his colleagues. Pro-Buddhist demonstrators smashed the United States Information Service libraries in downtown Saigon and the central Vietnamese town of Hue. There were rumors that the Armed Forces Council, headed by Lieutenant-General Nguyan Khanh, might "do something" before the beginning of the New Year holidays.

Chief of State Suu and his journalist friends politely avoided the topics uppermost in their minds. They exchanged new year courtesies and talked of the more pleasant aspects of the coming national fete. Suddenly, the telephone on Mr. Suu's desk rang urgently. The Chief of State took up the receiver. The voice at the other end of the line was that of Lieutenant-General Khanh, who conveyed the information that he had just ordered the dismissal of the Houng Government.

Mr. Suu took the message calmly and with all the dignity and restraint he could command. He continued the chat with the newsmen but left the office shortly afterwards to receive two important callers—the French Chargé d'Affaires with whom he had fixed an appointment earlier, and the U.S. Deputy Ambassador Alexis Johnson who had come on most urgent business, to express his disappointment at the new turn of affairs in the country. An hour later Radio Vietnam announced that the Government had changed hands, Premier Houng was divested of his high political office, that the Armed Forces Council had acted "in the interests of national solidarity and the consolidation of the war effort." Simultaneously, the National Buddhist Center announced that the Buddhist leaders had ended their fast unto death.

It was a typical Saigon coup—of the bloodless brand. Talks of the impending coup were in the air for several days. But it took place smoothly and swiftly, without any visible signs of revolt. Troops kept the vigil at Government offices and the Vien Hoa Dao, where the National Buddhist Center is located. The Houng Government had to go; otherwise, the "matryrdom" of the fasting Buddhist monks would have caused a major upheaval. General Khanh, whose position within the Armed Forces Council was none too secure and whose relations with Ambassador Taylor were none too cordial, emerged again as Vietnam's man of destiny. But another and a bigger coup was in the offing.

While the war raged loud and long in the Vietnamese countryside and the Communist Vietcong intensified their campaign of murder and arson, Saigon busied itself with a fierce political battle. Mr. Suu was back at the Gia Long Palace as the Chief of State, to ensure a smooth change-over and avert probable legal complications. Mr. Houng sought temporary political asylum at the British

Embassy but went back home after a couple of days rest there. Caretaker Premier Dr. Nguyen Luu Vien looked after routine affairs of state, while General Khanh and the Armed Forces Council worked overtime to organize a new government. In the peculiar political transition in South Vietnam, in which the Armed Forces form the least unstable of the numerous unstable elements in the country, as well as in view of the exigencies of war, the military junta has dominated the political front since the November 1963 revolution and the assassination of President Ngo Dinh Diem.

Khanh's task was extremely difficult and delicate. It was impossible to find a suitable person for the position of the nation's Prime Minister—someone who combined ability, experience, and personal integrity with public confidence and the capacity to be subservient to the military junta, and at the same time, unite the numerous conflicting parties and interests and galvanize the nation in its struggle for survival. There just was no one who answered all these specifications satisfactorily.

The Armed Forces Council's first choice was Major-General Nguyen Van Thien, 36-year-old Second Deputy Prime Minister, and Commander of the 4th Army Corps. He first rejected the nomination, set forth conditions when the offer was pressed and finally bowed out of the contest. The caretaker Prime Minister, Dr. Nguyen Luu Vien, a Harvard economist, made the next try and gave up, as he could not muster the support of all the parties and factions. His main handicap was his long stay in the United States and the persistent reports that he still held an American passport. Major-General Tran Van Minh

(Little Minh) who became Chief of the Army Staff after Khanh's exit, did not even try. He rejected the offer outright, preferring to stay on in his military duty.

The fourth and final candidate was Dr. Phan Huy Quat, a former Foreign Minister, who accepted Khanh's offer and managed to draw up a list of Ministers after several days of discreet negotiations with the numerous political, religious and other elements and the all-powerful Armed Forces Council.

The Quat Government formally assumed office on February 16, 1965, replacing the 20-day caretaker government. Immediately, the prophets of gloom pronounced their verdict that the new government would not last longer than the caretaker government. But Dr. Quat, medical practitioner, revolutionary and diplomat, took up the challenge in all earnestness and in the true spirit of dedication to the national cause.

His Government weathered a major coup d'etat. It witnessed the climax of the struggle for power within the Armed Forces Council and the dramatic exit of General Khanh, who was responsible for nominating him as Premier. Luck, too, was on his side. Soon after he assumed office, the "new look" war started, with the bombing raids on North Vietnam, bolstering the morale of the army and the people. But the "new look" did not last long. Another political crisis swept Saigon early in June amid the crucial battles in Central Vietnam, and the Quat Government was forced out of power.

The political shifts in South Vietnam have beaten the record of France's Fourth Republic. The Quat Government, formed in February 1965, was Vietnam's seventh government in the fifteen-month period since the over-throw of the Diem regime. During this brief period, South Vietnam has had three provisional charters, all abandoned immediately after proclamation. And nobody has cared to keep count of the coups and counter-coups in those fifteen hectic months.

The series of conflicts and crises in Saigon was part of the legacy inherited by South Vietnam after the Geneva agreement. The period between the Japanese occupation of Indochina in 1940 and the turn of the tide against Japanese militarism in 1944 provided an opportunity for the development of Vietnamese revolutionary forces. Then came the anti-French war and the anti-Vietcong war—and the never-ending revolution.

Among the various parties and factions in southern and central Vietnam, the Cao Dai, a political sect which operated under religious cover, received special favors from the Japanese. Cao Dai's supreme leader, Cuong De, had sought asylum in Japan during the days of the French colonial regime but he was never allowed by the Japanese to return to Indochina. Pham Cong Tac, the wartime nationalist leader of the Cao Dai, was arrested by the French after Japan's surrender and sent to a penal settlement. Later, he went to Cambodia where he died.

Vietnam produced a wide range of resistance movements during World War II. The Japanese assisted and encouraged Vietnamese revolutionaries to resist the French authority in the countryside. The allies encouraged other Vietnamese resistance groups to sabotage the Japanese war effort. Among this category were the Democratic Party, the Kuomintang, the Vietnamese Revolutionary

Party, the Hoa Hoa resistance movement—and the Communists.

In the confused period between Japan's surrender and the Geneva agreement, there also emerged in Vietnam a number of political hoodlums, with large private armies, wielding enormous power in certain localities. The most notorious among them was Saigon's Al Capone, Bay Vien, who controlled the slums, brothels, opium dens, gambling establishments, and the vast river traffic in and around the capital.

It was amidst this chaotic state of affairs that South Vietnam found its independence and chose Ngo Dinh Diem as head of the Government.

The Diem regime failed to provide the leadership that South Vietnam required during the vital period of transition. Diem acted courageously in destroying the Bay Vien gang but, unfortunately, he applied equally ruthless tactics in dealing with all opposition and all elements critical of his policy. The overthrow of Diem did not, therefore, solve the problem of popular and effective leadership. The military junta, which led the anti-Diem revolution, dominated the political front but it has not thrown up a leader of the caliber required for South Vietnam. Besides, the Armed Forces Council has been riddled with differences of opinion and personality clashes, leading to frequent coups and counter-coups. Nevertheless, the armed forces still constitute the only cohesive unit of power in Vietnam.

Vietnamese liberals insist that it is the absence of a legal and constitutional government that is responsible for the political instability in the country. In the absence of legality, there would be no order, and hence no stability. Under the ill-defined working system existing today, the Generals and the Chief of State share the power, while the responsibility rests on the shoulders of the Prime Minister. Few members of the Government have any political backing. At best, it is a compromise cabinet. But the compromise has endured longer than expected.

The long-term remedy to Vietnam's political instability might be a general election, for which the country is not ready. The military situation is hardly auspicious for a nationwide poll. Besides, Vietnamese parties are not organized on the basis of political ideology.

The Buddhist movement is a comparatively new phenomenon, that arose from the intolerant dictatorship of the Diem regime. Although nine million out of Vietnam's population of fourteen million are Buddhists, the Buddhist movement leaders have never expressed any political ambition, though they have been shouting political slogans, staging political demonstrations, delivering political sermons, committing political suicides. It was the Buddhist agitation that brought about the downfall of the Houng government. The leaders at Saigon's Vien Hoa Dao, humble scholarly monks, have emerged as a formidable political force in Vietnam. But, just as the Generals do not wish to assume direct political power, there is little likelihood of the Vien Hoa Dao leaders contesting the elections under the banner of an organized political party. They would rather influence and manipulate Governments and they are confident of their strength to fill this role effectively.

Religious sects like the Cao Dai and Hoa Hao do not

operate as political organizations. The (nationalist) Kuomintang Vietnam and the revolutionary Dai Viet parties have disintegrated into too many factions and groups, based on regional loyalties and personal preferences. A few former members of these political organizations are included in the Quat government but the party machinery is almost beyond repair.

Since March 1965, however, the Dai Viet Party, which has been in existence in one form or another since 1939, has been endeavoring to stage a comeback to the Vietnamese political scene. It is strongly anti-communist, claims a large number of members and sympathizers among the armed forces, and favors all-out war, with American military and economic aid. The Dai (Great) Viet party, as its name implies, is pledged to the restoration of national prestige and the unification of the two regions of Vietnam into a single nation. The Dai Viet leader, Ha Thuc Ky, has been resistance leader, anti-Diem campaigner, political prisoner and, for a brief period, Minister of the Interior in the Khanh Government. He is the only politician in war-time Vietnam to come out with a serious political manifesto and program of action.

Meanwhile, the muddle continues on Vietnam's civilian front, though there have been signs of hope since last February. The leaders and people in Saigon have recovered a genuine interest in the war. The so-called Peace movement has gone into eclipse; even the Buddhist leaders have disowned it. The call was for an immediate ceasefire, negotiations with the Vietcong invaders and an end to all foreign intervention. The Quat government met this baffling challenge, widely suspected to have been inspired by Vietcong propaganda, with astute statesmanship. The Premier argued that peace negotiations with the communists were just not feasible at the most crucial turn of the war, while the cessation of resistance, without firmly established pre-conditions, would be suicidal for South Vietnam. The new and more vigorous trends in the military operations seemed to have heartened the people. And the feeble plea for peace turned into an urgent cry for victory.

The post-Khanh Armed Forces Council has a new and healthy look. It is a junta of commanding generals, who bear the brunt of the war. Presumably to assure harmony and unity, the junta has no chairman; no single man enjoys a predominant position. The result is that coup rumors have been scarce in Saigon for some time. Nobody is likely to succeed in a military take-over bid; and one or two of the young generals, determined to win the war, have set themselves up as coup-breakers. Towards the middle of May, the Armed Forces Council decided to dissolve itself, presumably as an affirmation of confidence in the civilian Government. But the Generals were back again in the saddle of political power, after the fall of the Quat Government in June.

The Vietnamese political front lacks all the ingredients of counter-insurgency for winning the hearts and minds of the population. These include a good strong government, the rule of law throughout the country, and one cohesive plan of action. South Vietnam has to secure these fundamental requirements to inspire the people and to reap the full benefits of all the self-help projects and the vast economic aid obtained from the United States.

According to some Vietnamese leaders, the manifestation of what is described as political instability in the country is an inescapable phase of the current transition. It is part of the "growing pains" of a nation that emerged from colonialism to a long spate of conflict and chaos. They argue that the very fact that South Vietnam has survived so many bitter ordeals and the horrors of a series of wars is an unmistakable indication of its developing political maturity. It is a grim and tough way to maturity and wisdom, they agree, but add woefully "After all, Vietnam has been more unlucky than most other nations in the region."

Any government in Saigon is bound to be weak and fragile until someone comes along with the ability to assume responsibility and impose himself by force of personality, by political adroitness, by being able to identify and develop some basic Vietnamese common denominator. It is only such a leader who will bring the intangible asset of authority and acceptance by the people.

CHAPTER 5

The Long Gory Trail

The very existence of Vietnam as a separate country, and the survival of the Vietnamese as a distinct people, must be regarded as a miracle, for which scores of historians have so far tried vainly to find a satisfactory explanation.
Joseph Buttinger (*The Smaller Dragon*)

THE VIETNAMESE are small in stature. Most of them are thin and wiry, particularly the womenfolk. You seldom find a fat or flabby man or woman. They are generally active and agile and look remarkably healthy, in spite of the ravages of war and the inadequacy of medical aid and social services. They are intensely proud, acutely sensitive, almost on a par with the people of nearby Thailand. They like the good things in life and have evolved a philosophy which forms a judicious mixture of the "never mind" attitude and an uncanny faith in themselves and their national destiny.

It is difficult for the western-oriented mind to understand the Vietnamese people. In the midst of the fateful war and the urgency of winning it, many Americans think, and complain, that the Vietnamese are not pulling their weight, that they are indolent and obstinate. This, with the frequent internal squabbles and the insidious Vietcong propaganda, has led many people to believe that the Vietnamese people do not have their heart in the anti-Vietcong war, that they are tired and frustrated and prepared for peace at any price.

In Korea fifteen years ago, when the war was going in favor of the communists, many Americans and others in the United Nations forces thought likewise, that the South Korean people were not interested in the war, that it was essentially an American war, instigated and led by the late General MacArthur, and that the world should have left the Koreans, north and south, to work out their own destiny. The post-war story of Korea belies this theory in emphatic terms. In Saigon, I have met, and talked to, many Vietnamese including some of the peace advocates, who lament the tragedy that befell the MacArthur strategy in the Korean War. If communist aggression had then been dealt with effectively, they claim, there would have been a unified Korea—and no communist aggression in Vietnam.

The Vietnamese, like the Thais further west, are slightly different from the other inhabitants of Indochina. The Laotian people in the north are gentle, gracious and extremely courteous, firm believers in "ahimsa," the cult of non-violence. The war in Laos, unwittingly caught in the vortex of the big power struggle, has always been unique. Never has so much ammunition been used to so little purpose as in the war in Laos. The battle of Vientiane and the battles of the Plain of Jars, which I covered, were classics of this type of phoney warfare. It is the North Vietnamese communists who have done much of the active fighting in Laos.

The Cambodians across the Vietnamese frontier, in spite of the sound and fury of Prince Norodom Sihanouk's protests, are a mild-mannered, God-fearing people, also wedded to the Buddhist tenets of "ahimsa." Prince Sihanouk's special brand of neutrality and non-alignment, with the resultant appeasement of the communist bloc, forms a Cambodian adaptation of the thought that inspired India's Jawaharlal Nehru immediately after Indian independence. Perhaps, like Nehru in the winter of 1962, Sihanouk may some day confess that he has been living in a "dream world." He probably realizes the magnitude of Cambodia's stake in the Vietnam War. But, like the calculating neutral, he is inclined to be benevolent towards the belligerent considered more likely to survive the fateful struggle. Like all other non-communist advocates of peace at the communist price, he seems to believe that it is safer for all Asia to stay on good terms with the red giant in Peking.

Prince Sihanouk has often said that, in Cambodia, the people are backward, while the leadership has been progressive and intelligent. In South Vietnam, perhaps, it is the other way round. Even under French rule, the people and rulers of Cambodia and Laos considered the Vietnamese people as more alert and progressive than their leaders. Vietnamese had migrated in large numbers to Pnom Penh and Vientiane, as well as to the smaller towns in Cambodia and Laos, and settled down in business and professions, in active competition with the local people.

In the 14th century, Vietnam was a small tract along the coastline, with its southern point somewhere south of Hue, near the location of the present Da Nang Base, while the Khmer kingdom of Champasak extended to virtually all of South Vietnam, including the great Mekong Delta. By the middle of the 19th century, however, the Vietnamese empire spread south and west, reducing Champasak to a tiny principality, and covering a large portion of what is now Sihanouk's Cambodia.

That is the background to Cambodia's ill-will towards Vietnam. It arises from an emotional complex, almost similar to Cambodia's peculiar complex in dealing with neighboring Thailand, because large areas of the former Khmer kingdom were once under Thai sovereignty, ruled by a Viceroy of the King of Thailand. Even as recently as 1940, Thailand's late premier Marshal Phibun Songkhram conquered parts of French-protected Cambodia and held them for more than five years.

The Vietnamese, like the Thais, are originally of Chinese stock. Unlike the Thais, who have maintained their independence throughout the era of western colonization in Southeast Asia and before it, the Vietnamese have been influenced by a series of Chinese invasions and frequent periods of Chinese domination. For centuries, the main pre-occupation of the Vietnamese was resistance against the long line of would-be conquerors. That is why the existence of Vietnam as a separate country, and the survival of the Vietnamese as a distinct people, must be regarded as a miracle.

Strangely enough, in this respect, the only Asian parallel that suggests itself is Korea. Both Korea and

Vietnam happen to be partitioned into two distinct halves, professing two widely divergent ideologies, and belonging to two entirely different worlds.

It does not take us long to realize that the Vietnamese are about the toughest people in Southeast Asia, almost like the Koreans further north on the Pacific seaboard. For nearly twenty-five years, there has been almost nothing but war or preparations for war in Vietnam, and all the suffering and privation that go with it. For nearly two thousand years the Vietnamese have resisted, and revolted against, alien rule and alien attempts to subjugate them. To most Vietnamese, the present war is just another phase of the long-drawn-out campaign of resistance.

On the banks of the Saigon River, just a few yards away from the naval station, a twin statue is dedicated to the Trung Sisters, Vietnam's Joans of Arc, commemorating the first known revolt against Chinese domination in 43 A.D. The statues were built during the Ngo Dinh Diem regime and one of the Trung Sisters, cast in the image of Madame Ngo Dinh Nhu, then the self-styled "first lady" of Vietnam, was torn down by a violent mob after the coup d'etat which ended the Ngo Dinh rule.

According to Vietnamese legends, the Trung Sisters led their armies in a heroic revolt against the Chinese rulers and, when their forces were finally routed by the enemy, the sisters plunged to their death in a river in North Vietnam. Ever since, the Vietnamese people have regarded the Trung Sisters as symbolic of Vietnam's resistance to alien domination. Even as the communist Vietcong elements attempted to close in on Saigon and other centers of South Vietnam early this year, the Vietnamese people paid their homage to the Trung Sisters and sought their inspiration and blessing in the latest war of resistance against alien aggression.

Three times the Mongols have invaded Vietnam and, each time, the Mongol hordes were cut to pieces by the Vietnamese resistance forces. As a result of the long Chinese domination, Vietnam absorbed many facets of Chinese culture, Mahayana Buddhism imported through China, the Confucian philosophy and the emperor cult. But Vietnam has always resisted Chinese domination and has remained a turbulent state for centuries.

According to Chinese chronicles, the entire territory south of the Yangtze River was originally inhabited by the "hundred yueh"—tribes which had been completely absorbed by the Hans after the ruthless conquests of the 3rd century B.C. It would seem that ancient China's concept of the hundred yuehs was similar to Mao Tze-tung's idea of a hundred flowers, only one of them designed to survive. Some of these so-called hundred tribes south of the Yangtze were people of Malay/Indonesian origin and Mao might well quote history to lay his claim to all Southeast Asia, including Comrade Sukarno's sprawling domains almost touching Australia.

The Vietnamese believe that their ancestors formed one of the hundred yueh but miraculously escaped the fate that overtook the tribes which became totally integrated into the Han culture of China. The Vietnamese are proud of the fact that they were the only one of the hundred yueh that successfully resisted the process of "Hanhwa"—Sinification.

Vietnamese patriots recall, with surprise and disgust, that even in the 20th century, leaders of the caliber of Dr. Sun Yat-sen regarded the Vietnamese as prospective victims of Chinese domination. They quote Sun Yat-sen as saying that the Vietnamese are "slaves by nature" because they went under French rule after the exit of Chinese influence. They know that Mao Tze-tung is not likely to be more magnanimous than Sun Yat-sen in his attitude towards China's neighbors, particularly the last and most obstinate of the hundred yueh in the coveted Nanyang (southern) region.

Vietnamese in general regard China as their traditional enemy. There have been fifteen Chinese invasions in two thousand years, and a thousand years of direct Chinese rule over Vietnam. At the same time, there have been Vietnamese kings, rebels and revolutionaries who have sought China's military assistance when faced with internal unrest or external aggression. On these occasions, the Chinese came into Vietnam with large armed forces and occupied the country, refusing to leave until they were driven out by a subsequent revolution. Naturally, fear and suspicion of Communist China are strong and widespread among the Vietnamese people, including those in the communist north.

According to Ho Chi Minh, who has sought and accepted the assistance of Mao Tze-tung in his rise to power, "the Chinese and the Vietnamese people have always been friendly; it was the Chinese feudalists who were the enemies of both." The majority of Vietnamese intellectuals will not accept this simple thesis, nicely twisted to meet the current expediency. But there is no place for thinkers in Ho's Vietnam.

The French colonization of Vietnam was hesitant. Like the British in India and the Southeast Asian region, they first came as traders and missionaries and stayed on as rulers and protectors. The Vietnamese, who had just begun expanding their domain over the Indochina Peninsula, resented the advent of French colonialism. In 1851, Emperor Tu Duc, who ruled over Annam from the imperial capital at Hue, denounced the French as "barking like dogs and fleeing like goats." He ordered French traders and missionaries to be seized and thrown into the sea, with stones around their necks. Tu Duc lost his empire as the price of his patriotism.

The first direct French intervention in Vietnamese affairs came almost on the same pattern as the British intervention in India. This was in 1787 when the French signed a treaty with a dethroned Vietnamese prince, promising him military assistance in return for territorial concessions. The revolution in France intervened and the pledge was not fulfilled.

Almost until the middle of the 19th century, the French seemed unwilling to undertake the conquest of Vietnam. By that time, French policy had undergone a drastic change. The rivalry between European colonial powers reached its zenith. France was apparently spurred by considerations of national prestige and a systematic colonial policy was adopted. Advocates of imperialism in Paris dreamed of strengthening France's position, not only in Vietnam, where they had secured a foothold, but throughout the Far East, so that they could be assured of an eventual share when it came to dividing the colonial spoils in China.

Southern Vietnam, Cochin-China, with Saigon as its seat of power, was occupied by the French in 1859, Tonkin in the north in 1882, and Annam in central Vietnam in 1884. The adjoining kingdoms of Laos and Cambodia became protectorates of France a few years later and, before the end of the 19th century, the Union of French Indochina covered the entire peninsula and bits of territory squeezed out of neighboring Thailand in a series of diplomatic coups, effectively backed by French troops at the borders and gunboats in the Gulf of Siam.

French colonial rule, however, found no peace in Vietnam. In Laos and Cambodia, where French colonialism worked in the guise of protection, it had a more comfortable existence. The French controlled the country, with the ruthless despotism of the Sûreté, the despised loyalty of the Foreign Legion and the frightful political prison on Condor Island. French diplomacy and statesmanship made political converts among the Vietnamese elite. French missionaries and educationists claimed more converts among the Vietnamese intelligentsia. But the Vietnamese people, in all walks of life and political persuasions, planned and plotted to throw them into the sea, as desired by Emperor Tu Duc.

The Russo-Japanese war at the turn of the century, the revolution in China and the fall of the Manchu Empire, the outbreak of World War II, Hitler's blitzkrieg and the defeat of France in 1940, the subsequent deal between the Vichy government and Japan, whereby Japanese forces were in occupation of Indochina long before

Pearl Harbor—all these and the traditional Vietnamese spirit of resistance helped shape the inevitable uprising against French colonialism in Indochina.

That revolution hit its climax in mid-August, 1945, after the defeat of Japan, with the proclamation of Vietnamese independence in Hanoi and the beginning of a nine-year war which ended at Dien Bien Phu, and the total rout of the French colonial forces.

It was during this war in North Vietnam that the Chinese communists, under the leadership of Mao Tze-tung, swept into power in Peking. The communist conquest of China hastened the end of the war in Vietnam and the victory of the Vietnamese Lao Dong (Communist) Party.

The hero of that epic saga in turbulent Vietnam was Ho Chi Minh, a frail little man, with the wispy grey beard, the looks and mannerisms of a benevolent uncle, and the thoughts of—Mao Tze-tung.

CHAPTER 6

Southward Ho!

*We have sometimes been weak, sometimes power-
ful, but at no time have we lacked heroes.*

Emperor Le Loi

VIETNAM'S EMPEROR Le Loi waged a ten-year war of
independence against the Chinese conquerors of Vietnam
in the fifteenth century. His call to Vietnamese heroism
was part of the royal proclamation in 1418. The response
was lauded in Vietnamese verse and song and Le Loi
emerged as the victor after a long and bitter struggle.
There has been no shortage of heroes and martyrs in
Vietnam since then, particularly in the war of independence against French colonialism in the twentieth century.

The French conquest of Indochina was complete by
1884. From that year, the name of Vietnam disappeared
from the map. The French partitioned the territory that
was Vietnam into three regions, each with a different
administrative status. The new regions were: Tonkin, the
northern part with Hanoi as the capital; Annam, the
central area, with Hue as the capital; and Cochin-China,
in the south covering the Mekong Delta, with the adminis-

trative headquarters in Saigon. The people of Cochin-China were French subjects and enjoyed a relatively more liberal regime than the Tonkinese or the Annamese, who were designated as French protégés. Laos and Cambodia became French protectorates, ruled by their respective kings who, in their turn, came under the control and tutelage of the French Residents.

The anti-French resistance was all along concentrated in Vietnam, though the revolutionaries had supporters and sympathizers in Cambodia and Laos. Throughout the French colonial period, armed revolts against the regime rarely ceased and, between spates of violent agitation, there were non-violent campaigns. There were monarchist movements, the scholars' movement, the pan-Asia movement and, finally, the nationalist movement. Some Vietnamese patriots went into exile in Japan; others joined the Chinese nationalist movement; yet others established themselves in Hong Kong and elsewhere to promote the cause of Vietnam's independence from French rule.[1]

Most of these heroes have been forgotten, amidst the hectic developments since the end of World War II. But one that wrote his name in letters of red in the chequered annals of Vietnam is Ho Chi Minh, the man behind the Vietcong forces in their bid to take over the southern half of the country. Two generations of Vietnamese patriots had fought for their country before the advent of Ho Chi Minh. Their failures prepared the way for the communists, headed by Ho Chi Minh, to finally emerge as the liberators of Vietnam. The movement which began as nationalism, pure and simple, was captured by the communists, after a brief period of clandestine activity.

Many factors contributed to the communist success in Vietnam—skillful leadership provided by the Comintern, sound organization at the core of the party, the courage and determination of the party cadre. The communists attracted the idealist intellectuals through high-sounding slogans, and the under-privileged masses through their promise of a short-cut to better living standards. For the realization of their strategic objectives, the communists frequently changed the name of their movement, to suit the shifting political tempo of the land. The author of this epic campaign is Ho Chi Minh.

Today, perhaps, he is engaged in an agonizing re-appraisal of his association with the comrades in Peking and Moscow, amidst the crashing of bombs around him. But his place is secure in the history of Vietnam.

The name of Ho Chi Minh was heard by the Vietnamese people for the first time in August 1945, immediately after the surrender of Japan, in the proclamation of independence by a resolution of the Vietminh (nationalist) party. The Hanoi newspapers published the composition of the newly-formed provisional government, which listed Ho Chi Minh as the President. It was a strange name. Many Vietnamese thought it must be a pseudonym. Literally, it meant "He Who Aspires to Enlightenment." It was common knowledge a few days later that Ho Chi Minh was none other than Nguyen Ai Quoc, father of the Vietnamese Communist Party and mystery man among Vietnamese revolutionaries.

Ho Chi Minh, who turned 75 in May 1965, is descended from a long line of scholars who were, for the most part, junior mandarins and petty landlords. His father, a small-time rebel, spent several years in the prison island of Condor and was later placed under house arrest in Saigon, where he earned a meager living as a practitioner in Chinese medicine.

Ho, the youngest child of the family, started life as a teacher at the age of 17. He gave up the job after a year, went to Saigon to meet his father and, armed with a letter of introduction to a nationalist friend of his father in Paris, sailed for Marseilles as a cabin boy on the S.S. *La Touche-Treville*.

Ho's first rebellion was against his father's friend, veteran nationalist Tran Chu Trinh, who talked to the young firebrand in terms of dominion status for Vietnam and friendly co-operation with the French. Ho's stand was different. He would not settle for anything less than complete independence and the expulsion of the French from Vietnam. He was disillusioned by the views of the old nationalist, whom he left soon, to resume his job as cabin boy on international liners, travelling all over the world, to America, Africa, Europe and Asia.

When Ho Chi Minh went ashore, it was to work in the kitchens of the Carlton Hotel in London, devoting his spare time to the Overseas Workers Union, an anti-colonial organization established by the Chinese and Indian workers. Under the auspices of this organization, Ho brought out a journal called "Vietnam Hon" (The Soul of Vietnam) and smuggled it to Indochina with the help of Vietnamese employed on ships sailing to Saigon and Haiphong.

After the end of World War I, Ho Chi Minh made a trip to Versailles in the hope of meeting President Woodrow Wilson of the United States and handing him a memorandum indicting French colonial rule and setting forth his eight-point program, demanding autonomy for Vietnam, democratic freedom, amnesty for political prisoners, abolition of forced labor and equality of rights between the French and the Vietnamese. The attempt to gain American support failed in 1918, as it failed again in 1945. And Nguyen Ai Quoc turned to the communists and Moscow.

In 1961, Ho Chi Minh gave his own version of this conversion: "In the beginning it was patriotism, not communism, which induced me to believe in Lenin and the Third Internationale. But, little by little, progressing step by step in the course of the struggle, I came to the conclusion that socialism and communism alone are capable of emancipating the workers and down-trodden people all over the world . . . There was in Vietnam, as well as in China, the legend of the magic bag. Anyone faced with a great problem would simply open the bag to find a ready solution. For the Vietnamese revolution and people, Marxism-Leninism, Socialism-Communism, is not a magic bag or a compass, but a real sun which lights the road to final victory."

Ho Chi Minh's quest for the red sun now began in earnest. He was in Moscow in 1922, in Canton in 1925, as a protege of Michael Borodin, who headed the team of Soviet advisers in China. While in South China, forty years ago, Ho launched the Vietnamese communist movement. When the split came between the Chinese Kuomintang and the communists, and the Borodin group made its exit, Ho Chi Minh went back to Moscow. Some time

later, he returned to Southeast Asia, with Moscow's brief-
ing, worked among the Vietnamese refugees in north-
eastern Thailand, organized a congress of revolutionaries
in Hong Kong. He rose in the world communist heirarchy
and was appointed head of the Far Eastern Bureau of the
Comintern, responsible for liaison between Moscow and
the various communist organizations all over Southeast
Asia.

The anti-French movement in Vietnam gathered
momentum but a communist-sponsored revolt on May
Day, 1930, proved a fiasco. There were meetings, demonstrations and hunger marches but the French called out the
Foreign Legion whose machine-guns were promptly turned
on the long marching columns. Ho Chi Minh was arrested
by the Hong Kong authorities and there were rumors that
he had died of tuberculosis. But the wily rebel disappeared
from the British colony and for some years nobody heard
anything about him. Then, in 1941, he reappeared in
Moscow. In the intervening years, he changed his name
many times. Among the aliases were Nguyen Ai Quoc,
Ly Thuy and Vuong Son Nhi, all invented by him to suit
his purpose at different periods of his career.

Soviet Russia's entry into World War II brought about
sweeping changes. Almost overnight, the communists became respectable in the allied countries—and even in
the colonies of the big powers, where communist leaders
suddenly found themselves out of the prisons and were
entrusted with the task of organizing the people's war
effort on a new and wider united front.

Ho Chi Minh was soon back in Vietnam, to unite the
nationalists and the communists, in a campaign against

the Japanese and the Vichy government, and to promote the allied cause. He was joined by his favorite henchmen, Vo Nguyen Giap and Dang Zuan Khu, both veteran revolutionaries. Khu, who had just returned from China, called himself Truong Chinh, was a keen disciple and admirer of Mao Tze-tung. Giap was a close student of the communist military strategy and tactics, though he made no public acknowledgement of his admiration for Mao and the Chinese Communist Party.

Guerilla training camps were set up at the China-Tonkin frontier. The first battalion of the Vietminh army was formed by Giap in the winter of 1944. It was then known as the Vietnam Propaganda and Liberation Unit. The frontier guerilla camps received the assistance of the American OSS (Office of Strategic Services). The Vietminh quietly extended its underground activities throughout Vietnam. The war was definitely going against the Japanese and the so-called liberation forces found considerable support among the people. According to Giap, his original force of 34 men swelled into several thousands in a few weeks.

Just a few months before the end of the war, the Japanese in Indochina grew suspicious of the French officials and ousted them from nominal control in the provinces. This helped Ho Chi Minh and his army to extend their authority and influence through the rural regions of north Vietnam. By July 1945, when Japan's surrender seemed inevitable, the Vietminh became bolder and large parts of central and south Vietnam passed under their control. By mid-August, Ho's forces began closing in on Hanoi. Ho Chi Minh set up a national liberation committee and proclaimed that the "hour has struck for an offensive on all fronts." Giap entered Hanoi in the vanguard of his liberation forces. The puppet government of Emperor Bao Dai, set up by the Japanese, collapsed in no time. The Vietminh provisional government took over.

The French civilian officials and security forces, disarmed by the Japanese and confined to their hotels and homes, were helpless. France had won the war but the French empire in Indochina was being taken over by a short little man with a wisp of a beard. The French colonial minions were flabbergasted by the appearance of this barefooted "native" in khaki shorts and open-necked white shirt to challenge the might of victorious France.

But Ho and Giap went ahead, racing against time. In the south, the British occupation forces were landing in large numbers to take the Japanese surrender. The French were also staging a comeback and the various religious sects and dissident nationalist groups were challenging each other, as well as the authority of the occupation forces. Confusion and chaos ruled Saigon. Vietnamese rebel elements attacked the French and killed several hundreds of them in an orgy of murder and arson.

It was the Chinese nationalist forces who were assigned to take the Japanese surrender in North Vietnam. The French Government quietly concluded a deal with Chungking, promising the relinquishment of France's extra-territorial rights in China and special treatment for Chinese nationals living in Vietnam. In return for this pledge, the Nationalist Chinese agreed to withdraw their occupation forces and hand over control to the French. Ho Chi Minh sensed the danger, staged a tactical retreat, reached a preliminary agreement with the local French authorities and led a delegation to Paris to negotiate some sort of self-government for Vietnam.

Ho knew that the projected negotiations would not prove fruitful and took the precaution of re-activating his guerillas in their mountain hideouts. The French, on their part, were merely playing for time. The Paris conference was never held, and French armed forces started pouring into Hanoi and Haiphong. French cruisers arrived in Haiphong and the French air force bombarded the Vietnamese quarter of the harbor, killing nearly 6,000 Vietnamese. That was the beginning of the end.

The Vietminh renewed the attack. Ho Chi Minh again linked up with Mao Tze-tung. His party and forces abandoned all pretensions of being a nationalist organization. They changed over to communist tactics. The mountains and jungles came first, then the countryside and the isolation of the towns, which were the final targets—the very same strategy pursued by Ho Chi Minh's Vietcong forces in their campaign in South Vietnam. The Vietminh adopted Mao's slogan of "overthrowing imperialism and liquidating the feudal landlord class." With this, they began rallying the support of the long-suffering peasantry.

Giap's army fought on. Tactics and popular support were more vital to him than arms and equipment. Most of the weapons used by the Ho Chi Minh army were either left behind by the Japanese or seized from the French, while arms from Communist China came in towards the later stages of the war.

At the height of the campaign, Giap's forces numbered

as many as 300,000—regulars, provincial troops and guerillas. Steadily, the French were edged out of the Vietnamese countryside, to the towns and the eastern seaboard. By 1952, the war was going against the French who held only the towns. And, finally, came the big defeat and disaster at Dien Bien Phu.

Nearly 16,000 French Union Troops were killed or captured in the war, including a general, sixteen colonels and some 1,800 other officers.

Ho Chi Minh's big military victory came on May 7, 1954. The next day, at Geneva, he scored a great political victory. Indochina was partitioned and French colonialism was on the way out.

All that remained for Ho Chi Minh was to wipe out the partition agreement and work for communist control of all Vietnam.

CHAPTER 7

The Legacy
of Chaos

Mot Nuoc nhne trong van quoc
Ngay sau lanh dao thi gioi la ky
                                    Vietnamese fairy

THE FAIRY's message was inspiring. It came to Doc Phu (provincial chief) Nguyen Van Tuong in his dream some time near the turn of the 20th century, when the Vietnamese people were on the lookout for political and spiritual guidance in their campaign against French colonialism. The pious Doc Phu was elated by the forecast made by the good fairy and founded a religious sect; the French would not have tolerated a political party.

The fairy's message was:

> The smallest among nations
> Will some day lead all nations
> That'll be the strangest
> Saga on this earth.

Doc Phu Nguyen Van Tuong claimed a million followers of the Cao Dai sect he established at the command of the fairy in his dream. He was succeeded by the sect's first Pope, Pham Cong Tae, whom the French promptly transported to a penal settlement. The Cao Dai revolutionaries fought the French and the communists. But the fairy's forecast remained unfulfilled, totally unattainable, particularly in 1954, after the exit of French colonial rule from Indochina, virtually throwing the country to the wolves.

The powers that evolved the Geneva agreement believed that they had settled the destiny of the former French empire in Indochina. Northern Vietnam, above the 17th parallel, went to Ho Chi Minh and communism. The southern portion became independent of French control. Cambodia's status as an independent nation, following a policy of neutralism in its international relations, was affirmed in Geneva. An uneasy coalition of rightists, leftists and neutralists took over the reins of power in Laos. An international control and supervisory commission, comprising India, Canada and Poland, swung into action to ensure that the terms of the Geneva agreement were observed by all the parties concerned.

While Ho Chi Minh's party cadre and liberation forces promptly got down to work, tightening their hold on the people of North Vietnam with the ruthless efficiency of the communist system, South Vietnam seethed with unrest and disorder. Ex-Emperor Bao Dai, still the playboy he had always been, formally inherited the political power abdicated by the French in South Vietnam, but there were many forces at work in the struggle for power that was taking shape. Saigon was a cesspool of corruption and malfeasance. A flood of piastres poured out of Vietnam into France. Profiteers and racketeers flourished. There were warlords and gangsters holding the nation to ransom.

There were wealthy men and influential sects maintaining their own private armies.

Independence dawned on South Vietnam amid disruption and anarchy.

Probably the most colorful among the warlords of Vietnam at the time of its independence was Le Van Vien, or Bay Vien, leader of the notorious Binh Xuyen—a "sect" that had nothing to do with things spiritual. Bay Vien was a big-time gangster, who preyed on the Saigon river traffic, bought concessions for gambling dens, brothels and opium dens, controlled whole slum areas and maintained a large army of greenclad hoodlums. He collaborated with the Japanese during the war years. His men led the brutal massacre of the French in August-September 1945. He was, for some time, an ally of the communists and, at the same time, a business partner of Bao Dai, with whom he was reported to have shared the profits of Saigon's biggest gambling den. In the confusion of May 1954, this swarthy, illiterate gangster was the uncrowned king of Saigon, owning a large fleet of river boats, half a dozen opium factories, a string of brothels—and a well-armed and well-equipped army of his own.

The Cao Dai and the Hoa Hao sects, which were also in the forefront of Vietnamese politics at that time, were entirely different from Bay Vien's troupe. There were probably about two million people professing the Hoa Hao faith, a reform school of Buddhism, founded about a hundred years ago by the Venerable Master Tay An—an ascetic highly revered by his followers, who mostly came from the provinces of Vietnam bordering Cambodia. The Hoa Hao organized its own armed force, initially to cope with the insecurity of the Japanese occupation period. Later, the Hoa Hao fought the communists as an auxiliary force of the French Army. The resistance continued even after independence and the advent of the Diem regime.

Diem crushed the Hoa Hao movement with force of arms, and captured and executed its leader, General Ba Cut (who assumed the name after cutting off one of his fingers in a vow to crush communism) as a traitor to the country. After Diem's overthrow, the Hoa Hao forces joined the national army and have been a strong element in the resistance against the communist Vietcong. Early in 1965, the Vietnamese Court of Appeal exonerated General Ba Cut, and the Government bestowed posthumous honors on him as a martyr to the cause of national freedom.

Followers of the Cao Dai sect, still a major element in Vietnam, have evolved religious and philosophical tenets with a universal touch. They worship God, the Buddha, Christ, Joan of Arc and Victor Hugo. Their symbol is the triangle, inset with the all-seeing eye. The Cao Dai organized a revolutionary corps and launched anti-French resistance in 1940–41. After the war, the Cao Dai forces split into two groups, both anti-communist. One group sought French assistance, while the other fought the communists independently. The Cao Dai have spread their influence in recent years and one regiment of Cao Dai troops, equipped by the Americans, controls a large area bordering Cambodia.

In 1954, the Hoa Hao and Cao Dai might have been useful allies of any government that came to power in independent Vietnam, while Bay Vien and his gang were a disgrace to the country. There was, however, no acceptable element to fill the power vacuum left by the French withdrawal. That was the prelude to the tragedy of South Vietnam.

Bao Dai's Francophile henchmen were a thoroughly discreditable lot. Gangster Bay Vien was unthinkable. The Hoa Hao leader or the Cai Dai Pope did not qualify for national leadership. The Vietnamese army was totally demoralized and many units went over to the victorious Viet Minh, just as entire divisions of Kuomintang troops joined Mao Tze-tung when it was clear that Chiang Kai-shek was losing the war against the communists.

Bao Dai and the French would have liked one of their proteges to assume the premiership of the new state but that would have caused a major revolution immediately after independence. So the choice fell on Ngo Dinh Diem. He was the only acceptable candidate within the range of anybody's vision at that time.

Diem was a leader in his own right, although he was out of the political picture in Vietnam for some years. The Ngo Dinh's were one of the oldest families in Central Vietnam. By tradition, by individual ability and through the Confucian sense of duty, members of the Ngo Dinh family had a secure place among the mandarins of the imperial court at Hue. With the advent of French missionaries, the Ngo Dinhs accepted the cross of Catholicism. Diem's father, Ngo Dinh Kha, was a small-time mandarin who eventually rose to be the court chamberlain. Diem was the third of Kha's nine children. One of his elder brothers, Ngo Dinh Thuc, studied for the priesthood and eventually became an archbishop and a power behind the scenes during Diem's regime. Another brother, Ngo Dinh Cau, was a terror in central Vietnam and amassed a vast fortune while Diem was in power in Saigon. Younger brother Ngo Dinh Nhu and his wife virtually ran the regime for Diem.

Opponents of the Diem regime, in later years, have bitterly denounced him. According to them he was a feudalist by birth and tradition, French by education, colonialist by administrative experience as Minister of the Interior and top mandarin under Bao Dai. They argue that, within this framework, he was perhaps able and honest, but he never had the mandate of the people as Prime Minister or President of Free Vietnam.

In spite of these initial limitations, and the subsequent record, Diem looked like a major asset to South Vietnam at its crucial hour in 1954. He was a brilliant student, a very successful official, a province chief at the age of 28 and Minister of the Interior at the court of Hue at 30. He had disagreed with French officials of the time and resigned his position. For nearly four years, he did not fill any public office. Towards the end of the war, the Japanese were inclined to grant independence to Vietnam and invited Diem to accept the transfer of power, but the Japanese were on the way out and Diem discreetly declined the offer.

Twice, Ho Chi Minh tried to draw him into the Viet Minh camp. Ho was interested in Diem, not for his political acumen or his administrative talent and experience, but merely as a suitable "front man" because he represented the large Catholic community in Vietnam.

In 1950, the Viet Minh pronounced the death sentence on Diem and, as the French authorities refused to extend their protection to him, he left Vietnam on an extended tour which took him to many countries in Asia and Europe and finally to the United States. In this exile, Diem believed all along that he would some day be called back to his homeland to mold its destiny. He received the call in June 1954, barely a month after Dien Bien Phu.

Politically and physically, South Vietnam was then in the most wretched shape. Roads and railways, telephones and telegraph services, irrigation works and power stations, had either been destroyed or fallen into disrepair, after five years of Japanese occupation and nine years of internal unrest and conflict. Many parts of the countryside were already under the control of local warlords and their armies or the communist Vietcong units.

The Binh Xuyen gang was in command in Saigon and Cholon. The Cao Dai controlled the country west of the capital. The Hoa Hao were in control along parts of the Cambodian border and some areas of the Mekong Delta. And the communist bands were almost everywhere. Amidst the clash of interests between the French and the Vietnamese at the time of the transfer of power, whatever was left of the civil service had fallen to bits. Even in the Sûreté, Vietnamese and French officers were fighting each other, and adding to the chaos and confusion was the problem of resettling thousands of refugees from the communist north, who were flooding the non-communist sector of Vietnam.

Diem was faced with an almost impossible task. There was Bao Dai, still the Chief of State, and the remnants of French influence. Diem was not sure of the loyalty of his army chief, General Hinh, for the simple reason that he was a former officer of the French air force. Exercising the authority of the mandarin, Diem quickly got rid of Hinh by sending him abroad. Then came the rift between Diem and Bao Dai, who enjoyed the support of the French. A move was initiated by Bao Dai and the French to hold a conference in Paris and an invitation was extended to Diem. He suspected a plot against him and declined the invitation. The next man out was Bao Dai himself. Diem organized a referendum, asking the people to choose between him and Bao Dai as Head of State. And he won.

Ngo Dinh Diem's task, however, had only begun. It was one thing to dispose of the unpopular ex-emperor; it was another to deal with the many militant forces around him. The various sects, with their private armies, were preparing for revolt. They did not relish anything like a central authority in the country. But Diem was ready for them and he acted with resolve and ruthlessness. In this daring move, he accepted the guidance of the family, particularly Ngo Dinh Nhu and Madame Nhu. He also felt secure in the loyalty of the refugees from north and central Vietnam, mainly Catholics, who were as anti-communist as they were pro-Diem, for it was he who had saved them from communist terror.

Diem went right ahead with what he regarded as his divine mission. He spared none of the warlords and sect leaders, Strengthening his army with remnants of the French-trained officers and men, and the new faithfuls from his native Hue, Diem ordered an assault on the Binh Xuyen strongholds. Nobody had any regard for the dreaded Bay Vien and his gang, and the people of Saigon and Cholon joined the assault against them. The retreating Binh Xuyen elements caused enormous damage, burning and looting thousands of shops and homes. The campaign lasted for weeks but finally the gang was crushed by Diem's forces.

Diem might have been more magnanimous in his initial victory and adopted a slightly different approach to the other elements with private armies of their own. But the man of destiny was on the march, destroying all opposition, determined to tolerate none. The Cao Dai resistance soon distintegrated, while the Hoa Hao was destroyed in a series of pitched battles in the delta and the frontier regions.

Before the end of 1955, President Ngo Dinh Diem and the leader of his "revolutionary committee," brother Ngo Dinh Nhu, considered themselves absolute masters of South Vietnam. American aid poured into the country but Diem had no use for American advice. He tolerated the work of the International Control Commission, set up under the Geneva agreement, but never regarded members of the commission as particularly welcome guests of his country. In less than a year after he assumed power, Diem rejected the Geneva idea of holding elections for the unification of Vietnam. His stand was that South Vietnam was not a party to the Geneva accord and was not, therefore, bound by its terms. Perhaps he knew he did not have much of a chance of victory in a contest against Ho Chi Minh.

The Ngo Dinh Diem rule set the clock back in South Vietnam. While Ho Chi Minh consolidated his position in the north, with the establishment of a police state and the ruthless use of communist methods, Diem tried to rule the south in the style of the grand mandarin, exercising his divine right. His brothers and other members of the Ngo Dinh clan, meanwhile, made effective use of his divine right for purely material advantages—power, money and personal aggrandizement, in total disregard of popular sentiment.

The qualities that helped Diem to suppress all opposition forces were courage and determination and the consciousness of his mission as Vietnam's man of destiny. It would seem that, like all autocrats, he believed he was always right, that he could do no wrong. There was no compromise in the mental make-up of Diem and his brothers. They followed their own version of the old Confucian system, regardless of the fact that they were in charge of the destiny of a modern nation, riddled with internal conflict and external threat, in the mid-20th century. The result was that the palace became the center of power. Whatever was left of the administrative system went into disuse. Provincial chiefs bypassed the cabinet and the army. Like the junior mandarins of old, they took orders direct from the President or, more conveniently, from Ngo Dinh Nhu and his henchmen.

People in Saigon hold different views on the relations between the Ngo Dinh brothers who ruled Vietnam for well over eight years. According to some, Diem was a glorified puppet, completely under the control of younger brother Nhu and his aggressive wife. It is said that he resented this situation but was unable to extricate himself from it. According to others, Diem enjoyed his role. He trusted on one, except members of the family circle. He leaned on Nhu for advice in all affairs of state. Nhu told him only what he wanted to know. Nhu convinced him that the Vietnamese peasantry had been won over, that the Vietcong resistance could be crushed easily, that it was vital to liquidate all opposition and stifle all criticism, for the success of the regime.

Early in 1961, on a news assignment in Southeast Asia, I had the privilege of an exclusive interview with the late President Ngo Dinh Diem. The Vietnamese officials who met me at the airport and gave me all the necessary assistance and facilities, were extremely polite and efficient. In fact, they seemed so eagerly concerned that they arranged such a tight schedule of visits and talks for me that I found little time to make any personal observations or study during my brief stay in Saigon. I had, however, heard hushed talks about the Diem regime's unpopularity, its stern tactics in dealing with the press, and the danger of an anti-Diem revolution by the army and the people.

I found President Diem a most charming and shrewd host. We talked of Vietnamese affairs in general, the trends in Southeast Asia, and the war in neighboring Laos which I had just left before coming to Saigon.

He questioned me closely about people I had met and talked to, outside those in the government, and asked what reports I had heard over "Radio Catinat"—a reference to the political gossip in the lobbies and bars of the large hotels on Rue Catinat, frequented by Americans and other foreigners. I replied in polite and evasive terms, vaguely endorsing his criticism of rumor-mongers, and asked the question uppermost in my mind. Would he comment on the general impression, spread abroad, that he was a dictator?

President Diem seemed slightly embarrassed for a few fleeting seconds. Then he regained his poise and countered me with a question: "Do I look like a dictator, now that you have been talking to me for nearly half an hour?"

It was now my turn to be embarrassed. I said, perhaps I had used the wrong term, but I had heard from many people who admired him that he ruled Vietnam and the Vietnamese people with a very firm hand, like a stern uncle.

Mr. Ngo Dinh Diem smiled, evidently pleased with my tactful retreat, and replied: "Stern? yes. But kind, benevolent, and for the good of the people who criticize me."

I mentioned this conversation to a Vietnamese journalist friend. His comment was: "That's the great Ngo Dinh Diem all right—all self-righteous catholic, the condescending colonialist, the infallible mandarin, and the king who can do no wrong, all rolled into one."

While Nhu and his security men tried to make South Vietnam safe for the Ngo Dinh family, the communists worked overtime to subvert the peasantry and undermine the influence of the Diem regime in the countryside. There were appeals for a more liberal political system but they fell on deaf ears. As criticism of the Diem regime grew louder, the President withdrew deeper into the family circle and further away from the Vietnamese people.

The situation became increasingly disquieting. Vietnamese intellectuals stepped up their attacks on Diem's medieval methods. The Americans attempted to exert pressure on the Government to revise its attitude towards its critics and the people in general. As a result, President Diem ordered elections in Vietnam in 1959.

With Nhu and his security men in control, the elections proved a farce. Independent candidates, disliked by the regime, got nowhere. Nhu took all precautions to ensure that they never got a chance. Many of them were subjected to intimidation and prosecuted for all sorts of fictitious offenses. A number of candidates in the Saigon-Cholon area had their nomination papers declared out of order. One or two who managed to get elected were nabbed by Nhu's security men on their way to the Legislative Assembly.

Diem was impatient with the Vietnamese people. He was critical of the Americans—diplomats, advisers and aid officials. Nhu's security men combed the country to stifle the leaders of public opinion who asked for a voice in the conduct of state affairs. The press was gagged and terrorized. There was no official censorship but any newspaper that criticized the regime was either closed down or attacked by organized demonstrators. Diem and Nhu considered foreign correspondents a nuisance, and the Americans were no exception.

Diem turned down all appeals for internal reforms to enable South Vietnam to cope with the increasing communist threat. In his role as Vietnam's man of destiny, he seemed determined to alienate the Vietnamese people.

The little nation that launched out as a showplace of non-communist endeavor in Southeast Asia was faced with disruption and disaster. And the good fairy's message seemed meaningless, not only to the Cao Dais but to the entire Vietnamese people.

CHAPTER 8

The Gods
That Failed

The truly virtuous man, desiring to establish himself, seeks to establish others; desiring success For himself, he strives to help others succeed.

To find in the wishes of one's own heart the principle for his conduct towards others is the method of true virtue.

Confucius

THE LATE Ngo Dinh Diem of South Vietnam has often been described as the last of the Confucians. But he seemed to have ignored one of the major Confucian teachings on "the method of true virtue." Had he followed the Confucian precept in designing the pattern of relations between his government and the people, Vietnam would have been a much happier nation today. There would have been fewer coups and crises, and Vietnam would have been able to deal effectively with the communist aggression that threatens to destroy it.

Until 1963, nobody outside Vietnam had heard of a Buddhist movement in the country. The Vietnamese people, with their admirable qualities of religious tolerance and capacity to absorb and adapt alien cultures without losing their own, were suddenly the focus of world attention because of a revolt spearheaded by Buddhist monks, adding to the complexities of an already tangled internal situation. The monks came into the limelight with their non-violent campaign of protests, demonstrations and acts of self-immolation, throwing millions into a frenzy of emotion that led to the rise and fall of governments, all because the Ngo Dinh brothers failed to find in the wishes of their own heart the principle for their conduct towards others.

Buddhism came to Vietnam early in the Christian era, through Tibet and China. In Thailand, Cambodia and other parts of Southeast Asia, it came direct from India and later became accepted as the state religion. In Vietnam, as in China before Mao, the religion practiced by the majority of the people was a combination of Buddhist tenets and the teachings of Confucius and Tao.

For centuries, China had dominated Vietnam. By the 10th century A.D., Vietnamese made expeditions into Laos, Cambodia and parts of Thailand, resulting in some changes in the practice of Buddhism in the country. The result is that Buddhism in Vietnam today is a unique mixture of the original Buddhist tenets, some of the rites and ceremonies in vogue in Thailand, Laos and Cambodia and the basic teachings of Confucius and Tao. Buddhism to most Vietnamese, therefore, is not just a rigid religion but a philosophy and a way of life.

There is no organized Buddhist Church, though nine million people, nearly two-thirds of the population, profess Buddhism. The entire countryside, however, is littered with Buddhist shrines. Monks wear saffron robes in the southern parts of Vietnam, while the brown robe is the common dress of the Buddhist clergy in the central and northern parts of the country. Villagers support the faith by reserving paddyland for the maintenance of the pagoda and the priests. The Vietnamese people call the priests "they" (teacher, master, preceptor), but the French styled them "bonze" and foreign correspondents have adopted the French style.

Throughout Vietnam, as elsewhere in Southeast Asia, the Buddhist monk is held in great reverence. The authorities have no power to touch a man in saffron or brown robes, whatever crime he might have committed before joining the religious order. The bonze and his spiritual guidance have always been in demand—at births and deaths, weddings, and the numerous ceremonies and rites, including the observance of death anniversaries. For centuries, the monks were engaged in social and religious services. They never interfered in politics—until the Diem regime roused them to action.

Basically, it was not religious bigotry that stepped up the Buddhist movement. It was a feeling of resentment against the way the Diem government gave preferential treatment to the Catholic minority, and the numerous economic and other benefits the Catholics enjoyed because of the government's policy. The cry of religious discrimination helped to amass popular support for the Buddhist movement, and its leaders exploited this advantage whenever an opportunity arose.

French missionaries who came to Vietnam with the traders and the early colonizers worked among the people in the towns and villages. They made converts, covering all strata of Vietnamese society, and a benign government helped them in their mission. Naturally the Vietnamese Catholics, favored by the clergy who also operated major educational institutions, received priority in the award of scholarships and opportunities for higher education. Gradually the Catholic elite became established in top positions in government, business and industry. The ascendancy of the Catholics and the apparent helplessness of the Buddhists encouraged the formation of militant sects, such as the Cao Dai and the Hoa Hao, which pursued political objectives under cover of religion. .

Under the Diem government, the Catholics of Vietnam received more favored treatment than they ever enjoyed under French rule. Most of the key positions in government were held by Catholics. Much of the American aid supplies, like food, clothing and farm tools, passed through the village church and went in bulk to the Catholics. The prevailing impression among senior members of the Diem regime, and to some extent even the American officials, was that the Catholics, especially those who came south as refugees from the north, were more dependable than the other sections of the population in the all-important anti-communist campaign. It was suspected that some of the Catholic priests were acting as secret service agents of Ngo Dinh Nhu.

Yet there was no visible religious animosity among the people of Vietnam. In almost every other street in Saigon there is a Catholic church. Near the famous Buddhist Vien Hoa Dao, on Tran Quot Toan Street, there are at least five Catholic churches. The people lived in harmony. But the Buddhist movement was well under way, and Ngo Dinh Diem and his associates never suspected its potential strength.

In fact, Buddhist awakening in Vietnam may be traced back to 1935, when a series of Buddhist associations established themselves in the then French Union states of Tonkin, Annam and Cochin-China. They started setting up primary schools and high schools. The war and the Japanese occupation helped the bonzes in this constructive effort. When the French came back, scores of Buddhist monks started going abroad for advanced studies. Clad in their saffron or brown robes, they went to Thailand, India, Japan, Britain, France and the United States.

In a few years, the monks who had known only how to recite prayers and conduct religious ceremonies counted among their number many who held Ph.D. degrees from the best-known universities in the world. They stepped up the literacy campaign and started delivering sermons tinged with politics. Eighty percent of the people of Vietnam are today literate, largely due to the Buddhist awakening.

President Diem and his advisers seemed completely unaware of these developments in their midst. Diem thought of the Buddhist clergy as he had known them during the French days—illiterate men concerned with religious rituals and seeking alms from the people. He overlooked the changes during twelve years and disregarded the potentialities of the movement. And then, suddenly, the war flared up.

The Buddhist confrontation against Diem began on Buddha Jayanti Day, 1963. It was the birthday of Lord

Buddha, celebrated throughout Vietnam, with prayers in the shrines and processions along the streets, the hoisting of Buddhist flags and the setting up of altars and lanterns at street corners.

At the ancient capital of Hue, where the celebrations were traditionally held on a grand scale, the Diem regime, in an attempt to curb the growing influence of the Buddhist movement, ordered the provincial authorities to enforce certain regulations under the martial law, whereby no flag except the national flag should be flown at any public function. Actually on that day, the streets of Hue were festooned with crosses and flags and huge portraits of Diem's archbishop brother Thuc who was celebrating the silver jubilee of his ordination as bishop.

The Buddhist leaders protested. The Venerable Thich Tri Quang (the Brilliant Mind) addressed the congregation and spoke of the injustice of religious discrimination. Later, vast throngs of people assembled at the pagoda to listen to a re-broadcast of the day's ceremonies by the local radio station. The broadcast, however, did not materialize. The local authorities had cancelled it on orders from Saigon.

There were protests again and Nhu's police and security forces promptly intervened to disperse the congregation, almost on the pattern of the notorious Amritsar massacre in India by the British military forces many decades ago.

Water hoses and tear gas bombs came first. Then the artillery went into action. Nine died, hundreds were injured. The Buddhists had their baptism of fire. But their cause flourished as never before.

Protest meetings and demonstrations were held in Saigon and all the provincial areas. At Saigon's famed Xa Loi pagoda thousands of Buddhists, men and women, gathered at a condolence meeting. While they knelt and recited prayers, someone in the crowd produced leaflets denouncing Ngo Dinh Nhu and his wife. In a few minutes, Nhu's special forces, armed with grenades and submachine guns, raided the pagoda and arrested the monks and as many of the congregation as they could lay their hands on.

The venerable Thich Tri Quang sought asylum in the American Embassy. Other monks scaled a wall and took refuge in the nearby offices of the U.S. Operations Mission. Diem and his henchmen, in their rage, denounced the Americans for harboring enemies of the regime.

The Buddhist confrontation soon gathered momentum, fanned by the spate of self-immolation started by Thich Quang Duc on Saigon's Van Duyet Street on June 11. This monk quietly sat on the pavement of the crowded street, poured a can of gasoline over his body, lit a match and silently went up in flames, with his hands clasped together in prayer, a martyr to the Buddhist cause. The incident shocked the world; there was trouble and turmoil in Saigon and all Vietnam. There were six more cases of self-immolation in quick succession.

It was said that Thich Quang Duc, before he burned himself, had vowed that if his cause was right, he would die with his face turned heavenward and his heart would not be burned by the fire that consumed his body. Many people claim that it was precisely what happened, that he died looking heavenward, and that his heart remained intact. Bonze Quang Duc's heart, recovered after the cremation, is said to be kept on display at Xa Loi pagoda.

Finally, President Diem called a conference between the Buddhist leaders and Vice-President Nguyen Ngoc Tho, a Buddhist, heading an inter-ministerial delegation. Suddenly, Diem and Nhu found that the monks were educated men, who argued points of law more ably than the government's legal experts, and discussed major national policies more intelligently than some of Diem's ministers.

The talks ended in deadlock. Diem cracked down on the pagodas. Partly to appease the Americans, who were getting restless over the Buddhist turmoil and its impact on the war effort, Diem ordered the formation of another Buddhist association, called Co Son Mon (Ancient Mountain Gate) with the help of some old-style bonzes prepared to take orders from him. The result was that the Buddhist agitation became more intense. Students, youth organizations and large sections of the people supported the Vien Hoa Dao leaders.

The campaign struck a deep emotional chord throughout the country. Many who seldom went to the temples before started praying and attending religious sermons. Vu Van Mau, Diem's Foreign Minister who is now Ambassador in London, was drawn to the campaign for the Dharma. He shaved his head and offered his resignation. Diem and Nhu told him that he could not resign because of the martial law but reluctantly allowed him to go abroad on a mission that did not enhance the prestige of the crumbling regime in Saigon.

Already, there were two abortive military coups for the overthrow of the Diem rule. In one of these coups, Vietnamese air force pilots flung 500-pound bombs in the left wing of the Presidential Palace, known to be occupied by Ngo Dinh Nhu and his wife. Madame Nhu, who was in her suite at the time, had a miraculous escape from death, though she sustained minor burns, cuts and bruises.

The Presidential bodyguard of crack paratroopers was strengthened. The President became increasingly alienated from the people. Political Boss Nhu ran the government with his security forces and prison camps. Madame Nhu, the boisterous first lady, tried to help as often as possible with tirades against the Americans, the Buddhists and the people in general and then went on a lecture tour of the United States. Archbishop Thuc was said to be busy collecting real estate holdings in Saigon and other cities and then took time off for a trip to Rome. Brother Can, in Hue, busied himself amassing a fortune estimated at hundreds of millions of dollars in plantations, shipping lines and various industrial enterprises.

The list of those who opposed the Diem regime grew longer and more formidable. Even the Generals moved under surveillance. The Air Force and paratroopers, who led the earlier coups, were suspect. The political elite either found themselves at the Condor prison island or suffered humiliating persecution by Nhu's secret service men in the capital and district centers. Diem and Nhu were always on the lookout for loyal men, mainly among the Catholics in Central Vietnam, but even the Catholics were split in their loyalty to the regime.

- Nevertheless, Vietnam thrived amidst terror and

tyranny. The Vietcong menace became increasingly acute in the countryside but Saigon bloomed into one of the showplaces of Southeast Asia. American aid financed the Diem Government. It trained and equipped the Vietnamese armed forces. American advisers helped the anti-Vietcong war. American assistance hastened the reconstruction of roads and railways, airports and harbors, brought about improvements in agriculture and launched a small scale program of industrial development in the country. Out of the vast flow of American aid, though, only a trickle went into such projects as agriculture and health. The land reforms, initiated by the Diem government, failed to make any tangible progress, whereas the communists got down to their own dramatic, ruthless land-to-the-tiller program in the Mekong Delta and other rich rice-growing areas.

President Diem was said to have been a close student of Mao Tze-tung's tactics and strategy, but he was either unaware of the communist advance in Vietnam or unprepared for any resolute action against the danger. Immersed in the chaos and confusion that dominated the national front, and anxious about the threat confronting his own regime, he was probably unable to concentrate on the "red signal of danger" that flashed across all Southeast Asia at that time.

The coalition in Laos had virtually collapsed and the communists were pushing forward. There were threats of unrest in the sensitive areas of north-eastern Thailand. Malaysia, south of Thailand, which had been of considerable help to Vietnam in its anti-communist resistance, was faced with President Sukarno's confrontation compaign, effectively backed by Peking, Hanoi and Pyongyang. Meanwhile, South Vietnam was a house divided against itself. The cities glittered with neon lights but gloom and grief pervaded the countryside.

The second phase of the communist blueprint for the take-over of Vietnam was in progress. Vietcong terror and murders sent panic into the villages, caused suspense and tension in the towns. While Diem and Nhu fiddled with making the country safe for the Ngo Dinh family, the fire was spreading fast.

CHAPTER 9

Coups and More Coups

The mortal moon hath her eclipse endured
And the sad augurs mock their own presage;
Incertainties now crown themselves assured
And peace proclaims olives of endless age.
                                        Shakespeare

THE REVOLT that had been brewing since the Buddha's birthday grew increasingly intense and widespread. In spite of Ngo Dinh Nhu's all-out vigil, and his network of spies and counter-spies, the military leaders were drawn into the anti-Diem rebellion. They realized that a change of regime was vital to the success of the anti-communist warfare. They knew also that any bid to overthrow the Diem government would have the backing of the people. And so the explosion came on All Saints Day, November 1. By next morning, Diem and Nhu were dead, and the eight-year mandarin rule of Vietnam by the Ngo oligarchy had come to a dismal end.

Again, it was a siesta hour coup. Most of the people of Saigon had retired for the after-lunch nap when the coup leaders struck. The operations were planned in perfect detail, and launched swiftly, suddenly and without the the slightest forewarning.

Vietnamese army units from the Delta area slipped into the capital and blocked the main road to the Tan Son Nhut airport in the outskirts of Saigon. Crack marine units soon joined them. Tanks and armored cars rolled into downtown Saigon, meeting little resistance on the way. In and around Rue Catinat (Tu Do Street) in the heart of the city, the rebel forces encountered stiff opposition. But the loyalists apparently did not have their heart in the battle and the marines seized the central police station and sealed off the sister city of Cholon.

One by one, the citadels of Diem's power fell to the rebels. The naval headquarters along the Saigon River surrendered without resistance. The radio station and communications headquarters were taken over intact. President Diem's force of bodyguards tried to put up a fight. They strung barbed wire around the Gia Long Palace compound and tanks and truckloads of troops flooded the streets.

The rebels immediately regrouped themselves for the battle, while the coup leader, Major-General Duong Van Minh, contacted President Diem on the telephone and gave him five minutes to surrender. General Minh offered safe conduct to Diem and Nhu but Diem hung up on him.

The battle around the presidential palace was soon in full swing. Radio Saigon, now in the hands of the coup leaders, announced: "The day the people have been waiting for has come . . . For eight years, the people of Vietnam have suffered under the rotten and nepotic Diem regime but now the armed forces have come to their rescue."

The battle raged all night. Fighter-bombers swooped down on the palace and were met by shellfire from the rooftop and naval guns in the river. Tanks churned up the streets, lobbing shots into the nearby buildings, smashing shop-windows and splintering the wayside trees. The presidential palace was criss-crossed by tracer fire. Mortar fire reverberated through the city. By dawn, the entire area around the palace was in shambles.

A little before 7 a.m. on the Day of the Dead, as most Catholics call the Feast of All Saints, a white flag was hoisted over the charred ruins of Diem's fortress. Three hours later, an army unit found the Ngo Dinh brothers in a Catholic church in Cholon. Donning the robes of the priesthood, they had escaped through the complex of underground tunnels in the palace compound. Soldiers bundled them into a truck and, when it arrived at the coup headquarters, Diem was found with a bullet through his head and Nhu had been beaten or stabbed to death.

Saigon went wild with excitement. Thousands of citizens stormed the battered palace, shouting "Freedom!" and "Long Live the Military Leaders!" Hundreds climbed aboard the tanks to cheer the troops. The mobs ransacked the big book store owned by Diem's archbishop brother Ngo Dinh Thuc. Others raided some of the pro-Diem newspaper offices. The people of Saigon went delirious, laughing and crying, waving flags and shouting slogans.

Meanwhile, thousands of Buddhists flocked to the pagodas to greet their leaders who had been released from prison. It was said that most of the Buddhist leaders accepted the revolt silently. There was little jubilation at the shrines, because of the violence and bloodshed that marred the take-over.

The man of the moment in Vietnam, after the successful coup that overthrew the Diem Government, was Major-General Duong Van (Big) Minh, a professional soldier with a hero's record. A product of the French colonial army, he rose from the ranks to lieutenant and later graduated from France's Ecole Militaire. He also attended the Fort Leavenworth General Staff College in the United States.

Big Minh came to prominence after the Binh Xuyen operations which he led. He also organized and led the fight to suppress the private armies of the Cao Dai and Hoa Hao sects. Diem promoted him to the rank of Major-General but grew suspicious of Big Minh's popularity within the armed forces, particularly among the younger officers, shifted him from one position to another and finally elevated him to the powerless post of Military Adviser to the President.

Big Minh was no political general. On many occasions, he turned down the idea of overthrowing the civilian government by force, so that the army might assume power and get on with the anti-communist war. He believed in properly constituted civilian authority and refused to get mixed in politics. Finally, he yielded to persuasion and pressure by his colleagues in the armed forces. Probably, he was also influenced by Ngo Dinh Nhu's efforts to make the military forces share the responsibility for the anti-Buddhist crackdown. Anyway, the Generals needed the popularity and prestige of Big Minh for the coup d'etat and it was impossible for him to keep out.

Big Minh's role in the anti-Diem revolt in Vietnam was similar to that of Major-General Mohamed Naguib in the Egyptian coup of 1952. Like Naguib, Minh was the ideal leader but the revolutionary junta in Vietnam, like that in Egypt, emerged as the supreme authority. And, when the working of the junta revealed the ambitions of some of its leading members, it was apparent that the coup would breed more coups, as it did in Egypt and elsewhere, though few people thought in terms of coups like the comic opera, especially in the context of the national emergency that faced Vietnam at the time.

One of the more prominent members of the revolution-ary junta was Brigadier-General Ton That Dinh, who had enjoyed the confidence of Ngo Dinh Diem and had successfully organized the resistance against the earlier coups. According to Saigon gossip, Dinh sought his reward after saving the Diem regime twice; he wanted to be named Minister of the Interior. Diem turned down the request and Nhu promptly sent Dinh's brother to prison on some flimsy charge. Dinh appealed to the President, who was unable to countermand Nhu's orders. The regime lost a key man in Dinh when he went over to the rebels with a vengeance.

The master mind behind the coup was Major-General Tran Van Don, who resented the high-handedness of Diem and Nhu in disregard of the sentiments of the armed forces and the people, and had organized the previous coup to overthrow the regime. But while Big Minh never tried to project himself as the nation's savior and Don went about reorganizing the armed forces and restoring public confidence in the new regime, Dinh started pushing himself as the originator of the coup d'etat. Many of the younger military leaders, though they were happy to use Dinh for the success of the revolt, had little confidence in him and resented his campaign of trying to establish himself as the man behind the coup. The rift within the coup leadership had already begun, and others, like Nguyen Khanh, picked up the cue.

The main political element to support the military coup was the Dai Viet Party, which had friends and sympathizers among the generals and colonels who organized the anti-Diem revolt. The leader of the Dai Viet Party, Dr. Nguyen Ton Hoan, was then in Paris and his followers desired that he be recalled to head the new government. Many of the coup leaders, however, did not want a drastic change, especially after the violence accompanying the revolt and its impact on world opinion. They wanted a "neutral" person to head the government and the choice fell on Nguyen Ngoc Tho, who was Vice-President under Diem. Big Minh, who had worked with Tho in his campaign against the warlords and their private armies, accepted the nomination of Tho as Prime Minister.

The new government announced its advocacy of a peaceful revolution, and the military leaders thought they had done their duty. The United States promptly restored the aid cuts, enforced a few weeks ago in protest against Diem's policies. Everybody thought the war against the Vietcong would now be stepped up, and that victory was around the corner. The United States even announced its plans to withdraw several hundred American servicemen from Vietnam, beginning in January 1964.

These hopes, however, remained unfulfilled. The communists stepped up the tempo of their offensive, not only in the countryside, but even in Saigon, where the new government had not yet been able to police the streets as efficiently as was done during the Diem regime. The Government in Saigon was being re-organized. The pro-Diem elements were being removed, while politicians from Diem's prisons converged on the capital with all sorts of ideas, and news-sheets mushroomed with many discordant notes in their new-found freedom.

After the first flush of enthusiasm, Saigon began settling down to the discontent and chaos which had become part of its normal life in years of strife and turmoil.

Big Minh, the professional soldier, found it difficult to cope with the political warfare that raged all around him. The Vietcong campaign was becoming increasingly dangerous and the program of resistance had to be re-organized speedily. Though none of the generals questioned his authority, the problem of keeping them together was formidable, especially as some of them did not fully share the motives that inspired Minh and his close associates.

The politicians set forth a hue and cry for general elections and, although both Chief of State Minh and Premier Tho conceded the need for early elections and a return to the democratic tenets, they were not certain that it would be a feasible proposition. There was a clamor for stern action against everyone who served under Diem but that would have meant complete dislocation of the government's functions. Revenge-seekers, witch-hunters and reward-claimers flocked Saigon—people with harrowing tales of life in Diem's prisons, people who denounced Tho as just another Diem stooge, people who clamored for a dynamic revolution, whatever that meant.

In three months, there was another coup, this time for the removal of Prime Minister Nguyen Ngoc Tho. This coup, which according to Vietnamese military leaders sought to purge the revolution of all undesirable elements in it, was headed by a senior colleague of Big Minh, Lieutenant-General Tran Thien Khiem. It was a quiet, bloodless coup, and Premier Tho bowed himself out gracefully.

Again, the Dai Viet Party proposed Dr. Hoan to head the government and, although he was recalled to Saigon from Paris, the revolutionary junta changed its mind. It was said that by this time the young Generals, having tasted political power, were in no mood to abandon it. The junta wanted someone who would be subservient to it and recommended Major-General Nguyen Khanh to the post of Prime Minister.

Khanh, who was one of the promoters of the anti-Diem coup, had been taking a leading part in the functioning of the military junta and most people thought that a good soldier as head of the government would be the proper answer to the peculiar problems confronting Vietnam at that time. Besides, he was far more acceptable than Tho, who still bore the stigma of his long association with the Diem regime.

The next phase was the Minh-Khiem-Khanh troika.

Minh, who stepped down from his position as Chief of State, was entrusted with the task of forming a High National Council, an interim legislative body; Khiem was Defense Minister and Commander-in-Chief, while Khanh became the Acting Prime Minister.

This time, in Saigon, the jubilation over the changes was slightly subdued. The United States, though increasingly aware of the crucial phase of the anti-Vietcong war and looking for political stability in the country, seemed elated to have a youthful, dynamic army leader at the helm of affairs in troubled Vietnam. More American aid began to pour into Vietnam and Defense Secretary Robert McNamara came out to look over the new regime and paid a glowing tribute to Khanh's leadership. It looked like a happy augury for the Khanh era.

The handsome soldier with the goatee emerged as Vietnam's new man of destiny. He believed he was endowed with the dynamism of Gamal Abdel Nasser of the United Arab Republic. Besides, he had a vague faith in the political sagacity of his neighbor, Prince Norodom Sihanouk of Cambodia. Beyond that, it was a case of greatness thrust upon him, though he picked up the tricks of the game with admirable speed and thoroughness.

For the time being, Khanh's problem was to consolidate his personal position. The task called for two major moves: the elimination of his seniors in the army from the local scene and the establishment of a military junta, with himself as its leader, to prevent further coups except those designed and executed by himself.

In a few weeks, Lieutenant-General Khiem was away on a special mission to West Germany, where he received

Prime Minister Khanh's orders posting him as Vietnam's Ambassador to Washington. He has been there ever since, and was the only senior diplomat who was not invited to the conference of Vietnamese heads of missions throughout the world held in Saigon in March 1965. This was presumably because his name was mentioned in connection with the anti-Khanh coup d'etat earlier in the year. Radio Vietnam, seized by the rebels, claimed that it was a coup by proxy, that Lieutenant-General Khiem would head the new government sponsored by the coup leaders. That coup proved a total flop and Khiem's exile continued, with added uneasiness.

Big Minh, the soldier with little political ambition, fared no better. His assignment to establish the High National Council was not meant to be successful. But even Khanh found it difficult to banish him from the scene with undue haste. Towards the end of 1964, however, Khanh managed to send out Big Minh as a special roving envoy to advance the cause of Vietnam to the non-aligned Asian and African countries—a mission from which he has not been released even after Khan's exit. In May, Big Minh tried to return home, but his plane was not allowed to land in Saigon.

The father of the coup was still in orbit, while more coups and counter-coups disfigured the brief but eventful Khanh era in Vietnamese politics.

CHAPTER 10

Khanh of the "Young Turks"

Saigon, Oh Saigon's a wonderful place
But the organization's a bloomin' disgrace;
There's captains and majors and light colonels, too
With hands in their pockets and nothing to do.
Dien Cau Dau, Dien Cai Dau
With hands in their pockets and nothing to do.
                                        Night club music.

THE WAG who composed and sang this telling piece for
the amusement of Americans and other foreigners who
frequented Saigon's exclusive night clubs was definitely
unfair to the Vietnamese army officers and men who bore
the brunt of the anti-communist war that raged all over
the country. But as the series of coups and counter-coups
rocked the embattled nation at frequent intervals and still
brought about no significant changes, there was widespread endorsement of the theme that the "organization"
in Vietnam was becoming a "bloomin' disgrace."

· Vietnamese coups and crises made world headlines
throughout 1964. The war had been going on for years.
It had cost nearly 100,000 Vietnamese dead on both sides.

The daily casualty list was mounting, as the Vietcong became increasingly daring in their aggression. There was a trace of despair among the men who planned the operations. They began talking in terms of a long, hard war— an almost endless war. The troops and their field commanders were restive. The Generals and their American advisers were not sure how long the war-weary Vietnamese morale would endure the strain of hopeless indecision. The situation was complicated by military elements that advocated a "Bac Tien" (To the North) movement, and civilian elements that favored the neutralist sentiment, including some even ready for peace at any price.

It was a challenging situation, in which discord and strife were the dominant features. The United States, which by now had staked its Asian policy on the outcome of the war in Vietnam, was getting impatient. All that Washington sought was a stable government in Saigon, so that the aid program and the military operations would produce some tangible results. While American policy in Vietnam gradually emerged from indecision and drift to determination and design, the Vietnamese political front became increasingly nebulous, if not altogether unpredictable. Washington's real part in the anti-Diem coup may never be known but it was well known that American interests had floodlit the way for the enemies of the Ngo Dinh rule, by every means short of direct involvement. And now the military take-over, hailed as a happy augury, became even more embarrassing to Vietnam's American allies.

The Government had no popular mandate. The change

was by no means peaceful or constitutional. Perhaps the exigencies of the war justified its prompt recognition by the United States, and the resumption of military and economic assistance. But the outlook became dubious when the Generals started playing politics, while the military crisis grew acute. In fifteen months, Khanh staged no less than five coups, including the one that placed him in power within 90 days after the overthrow of the Diem regime. He assumed office as President of the Republic but stepped down after a brief spell, as he found the position untenable. All these and more contributed to the political instability in Vietnam.

Though he was chairman of the all-powerful Armed Forces Council, Khanh did not enjoy the confidence of many of its members. Though he tried to win over the influential Buddhist leaders, they were not certain of his loyalty to their cause, especially after his henchmen arrested nearly 1,500 Buddhists in central Vietnam in July 1964. A running feud between Khanh and the United States Ambassador, General Maxwell D. Taylor, plagued Vietnamese American relations, though without seriously hampering the war effort.

According to one version of the story, widely current in Saigon, Khanh was extremely sensitive about his importance as the fighting leader of the Vietnamese people. He resented all advice and suggestions calculated to introduce political stability and some semblance of a liberal government in the country. Ambassador Taylor and his aides, in turn, resented this attitude of Khanh, who added fuel to the fire by openly denouncing the veteran soldier-diplomat as "unfit to hold the position of ambassador."

"If Mr. Taylor doesn't act more intelligently," he said, "the United States will lose Southeast Asia and Vietnam will lose its freedom."

On one occasion, Khanh addressed a public rally in Saigon and called for the "liberation" of North Vietnam by direct military action, though it meant the violation of the Geneva agreement. Ambassador Taylor promptly called on Khanh for an explanation of his statement and was politely assured by the young General that he had to offer the people some hope of ending the war and that the Vietnamese were studying plans for extending the operations beyond the 17th parallel. Yet, early in February, after the first American bombing attack on North Vietnam, Khanh demurred vaguely and then ordered the Vietnamese air force to join the air assaults.

To the Americans, as well as to most Vietnamese, Khanh was an enigma. The military leaders thought he was growing too fast, and was too cunning, self-willed and dangerous. The politicians hated him for the way he sought power and tried to retain it at any cost. The Buddhists believed he was merely trying to exploit their influence, while at the same time bidding for the support of the Can Lao (Catholic) movement. But Khanh held the center of the Vietnamese stage and was able to make and unmake governments at will because of his position as head of the Armed Forces Council. The last of his coup series took place on the eve of the Vietnamese New Year, when he dismissed the cabinet over the telephone, though it took him a fortnight to set up another government.

Amid the political confusion and tussle for power in Saigon, and the strained relations between Khanh and

Taylor, morale among the people and the armed forces was at a low ebb. The communist Vietcong exploited the situation effectively. They began the third phase of their tactics with mobile warfare and large scale raids on the big towns, probably preparing for the final showdown.

The Vietcong attack on the big American base in the town of Pleiku in central Vietnam was the turning point in the war. It coincided with Soviet Premier Alexei Kosygin's visit to Hanoi and U.S. Presidential Adviser McGeorge Bundy's sojourn in Saigon. From the country-side reign of terror and murder, the Vietcong had begun to concentrate their attack on the American bases and personnel. In Pleiku, they killed seven and injured as many as 109, besides causing enormous damage, including the destruction of a number of helicopters and reconnaissance planes.

American reprisal was quick. In a few hours, North Vietnamese military camps and staging bases across the 17th parallel were smashed by American bombers. The Vietnam war took on a new look. Next day, Khanh personally congratulated his air force commander and the Vietnamese pilots for their share in the bombing of North Vietnam.

Speculation over the next turn of events agitated all Saigon—except the coup-makers and coup-breakers. Would Hanoi, with Soviet and Peking aid, try to bomb military establishments in South Vietnam? Would Red China intervene in Vietnam and precipitate another Korea-type war? The questions remained unanswered but the tempo of the war heightened.

Revolution was still the dominant theme in Saigon.

Reports of the air strikes and the Vietcong attacks were eclipsed by rumors of another coup in the Vietnamese capital. And then, on February 19, a major political sensation rocked the embattled nation.

· It was a lightning coup, again during the seista hours of the afternoon.·For twenty-four hours the coup leaders and their forces were in control of Saigon, and it was belived that they had overthrown the regime of Lieutenant-General Khanh. By next morning, however, it developed into a bitter, multi-cornered struggle for power, in which there were no victors, but a wide range of vanquished. The coup flopped, but it ended the Khanh era in Vietnam. There was a counter-coup against Khanh by his own generals, and another leader who had tried to be Vietnam's man of destiny was out. ·

The coup was marked by a formidable show of strength, on land, sea and in the air. It revealed violent shifts in loyalty among the leaders of Vietnam's armed forces. There were moments when a major civil war seemed inevitable. But, barring a few minor incidents, it was an entirely bloodless affair.

, The coup was masterminded by a young Vietnamese colonel, Pham Ngoc Thao, who had been a mystery man in the city for some time since his return from Washington, where he was press attache at the Vietnamese Embassy. Thao, who went into hiding after coming to Saigon, suddenly emerged at the head of a fairly large force which struck with lightning speed, seized the airport on the outskirts of the city, the broadcasting station, the Armed Forces headquarters and all the important military installations. And then, he went on the air to announce that it was a coup by proxy, that his former chief, Lieutenant-General Tran Thiem Khiem, the Ambassador in Washington, would lead the Government replacing the Khanh regime. Thao said that Khanh had been dismissed and arrested. He called on all army units to rally to the support of the coup.

Precisely at that moment, General Khanh was flying out of Saigon to the Bien Hoa air base, about fifteen miles away, to seek the support of the young Air Force Chief, Air Vice-Marshal Nguyen Cao Ky. He had also contacted other army commanders and ordered resistance against the coup.

By dusk, Saigon looked like a city on the war front. Shops and stores put down their shutters. Dozens of sky-raiders were up in the air, buzzing low over the strategic centers of the city and its environs. Tanks and armored cars assembled at street corners and it seemed that the opposing military factions were headed for a showdown. Nobody, however, was able to guess whom the various armed units on the streets favored, as they changed sides quite frequently, depending on the fortunes of the rival parties.

Saigon citizens, no novices in the game of coup-watching, gathered on the streets and along the river-front. Many seemed thrilled at the prospect of a battle. They were impressed by the "show" which, they said, was far better than the fighting scenes in the films.

Somehow, the coup leaders found little support among the army units and their commanders. By next morning, the coup was virtually smashed. The city was recaptured by the loyalists. The rebel forces surrendered without resistance. Their leaders put on civilian clothes and got out of the capital in jeeps and helicopters. The Government of Prime Minister Quat, which had assumed office barely a month before and stayed silent for a day after the capture of Saigon by the rebels, now came out with a series of official statements and proclamations. It offered sizeable rewards for the capture of the rebel leaders, but promised amnesty to all army units which had taken part in the rebel campaign.

It was a happy weekend for the population of Saigon. The early curfew, imposed by the coup leaders, was gone, and the city returned to its normal life of glow and gaiety. Even the large corps of foreign correspondents thought it was time for a little relaxation after a hectic spell of work, without the slightest realization that yet another coup was in the making. The major topic of speculation at the bars and cafes was whether Colonel Thao's coup was sponsored or supported by Washington, because of the strained relations between Ambassador Taylor and General Khanh. The question, however, seemed irrelevant, in the context of the surprise that awaited them.

This time, it was a coup against General Khanh, not by any agent of the United States, but by the Generals who had just crushed the coup against him. It was a manifestation of the shifting loyalties and disruptive intrigues that riddled the Vietnamese political scene. The Americans in Saigon, despondent over the incurable instability in the country, kept absolutely silent about the coup and countercoup. Ambassador Taylor frankly told newsmen that he just did not know what was going on.

The young generals of Khanh's military junta, after

having suppressed the coup, held a meeting to consider the situation. They agreed, almost unanimously, that their ambitious chief was responsible for much of the disunity and conflict in the country. They resolved that General Khanh must go and communicated the decision to him, privately and informally, to the air base in the southern delta area where Khanh was officially stated to have been inspecting important military installations.

General Khanh was furious. He signed a decree dismissing some of the army commanders suspected of leading the revolt against him. He appealed to all the army units to rally to his support. Vietnam was confronted with the threat of a second civil war over the same weekend.

It was a hectic, behind-the-scenes drama, and the nation's destiny hung on its outcome. Khanh flew from the delta air base to the highland resort of Dalat in the north. He repeated the threats to dismiss the "young Turks" of the armed forces and send his tanks and paratroopers to take Saigon. But the Generals stood firm. This time they insisted that Khanh accept their "ultimatum" and quit gracefully.

That Sunday dawned uneasily in Saigon. Jet fighter-bombers had been flying over the city all night. The Generals were in conference throughout the night. Vietnamese military commanders and the men under them, in the distant towns and jungles silently debated major issues of loyalty and expediency. Then came the official announcement that Lieutenant-General Nguyen Khanh had been relieved of his post as Commander-in-Chief of the Armed Forces. It was an order signed by the Chief of State and counter-signed by the Prime Minister.

Khanh knew he was licked by his own men. Yet he seemed in no mood to give up the fight. The Armed Forces Council sent two of its senior members to Dalat to "negotiate" the "exit" terms with the ousted leader. But while the negotiations went on, a new commander-in-chief, Major-General Tran Van (Little) Minh (no kin of the exiled Big Minh) formally assumed office. If the coup was crushed and the coup leaders fled the country, the man against whom they conspired had also fallen by the way-side, stripped of his powers and sent away in virtual exile. By the end of the week, Khanh was off, as another Viet-namese ambassador-at-large, joining the two other lieutenant-generals whom he had sent out in glorious exile in his own rise to the political and military summit in the country.

I was at Saigon airport when they bid farewell to Lieutenant-General Khanh. It was a memorable scene, which added to the quaint mystery of Vietnamese politics and the unique mental and moral fiber of a people whose main preoccupation would appear to be in the line of discord and conflict.

Now that the squabble had been settled, Khanh went into exile with honors befitting a national hero and tears worthy of a dedicated martyr. There was drama, with a tinge of pathos, at the formal handing over ceremony at which Khanh relinquished office as Commander-in-Chief, as well as at the elaborate farewell function before he took off for Hong Kong on the first lap of his uncertain mission.

The tearful farewell and glowing tributes seemed in-congruous against the background of the bitter feud that preceded them. Air Vice-Marshal Nguyen Cao Ky, who broke up the coup but emerged as the leader of the campaign to exile Khanh, looked desolately peeved. Prime Minister Quat, who had turned down Khanh's insistent demand that he should resign with the entire cabinet, in protest against the young Generals' move, seemed equally solicitous.

Khanh himself contributed to the dramatic touch. As he boarded the aircraft, he took out a small plastic pouch and whispered loudly enough for all to hear: "This is the good earth from Free Vietnam." There was a bulge of black showing at the bottom of the small pouch which Khanh solemnly replaced in the breast pocket of his spotless uniform.

An American correspondant, completely lost in the mystery of the farewell scene, quipped "Either they're really sad he's going, or they're exceedingly good actors."

It is not easy to understand Vietnam and the Vietnamese people. But, if the world has misunderstood them and the trend of events in their country, they cannot be held responsible for it.

CHAPTER 11

The "New Look" War

Better betray others than be betrayed yourselves.
Tsao Tsao

AMIDST THE conflicts and crises that rocked Saigon at the beginning of 1965, the war became increasingly fierce and assumed fateful proportions. The largest combat military action since the Korean War flared up in Vietnam in February.

The latest American jets, as many as a hundred at a time, began roaring over communist North Vietnam in a relentless series of bombing and strafing raids. The South Vietnamese Air Force joined the aerial assaults. Carrier-based aircraft from units of the American Seventh Fleet supported the operations from Da Nang and other bases in South Vietnam. American naval units reinforced the coastal patrol, hunting down troops and arms shipments from the North to assist the Vietcong campaign.

At first it was at the rate of one big air raid of North Vietnam centers every other day. Then it became an almost daily affair. In a few weeks, except for a brief lull in May, the air attacks on North Vietnam were stepped up on a round-the-clock basis. Ho Chi Minh's military installations, training centers and staging bases were smashed. Radar stations, armament depots, highway bridges, railway yards and scores of other vital targets were either destroyed or severely damaged. For the first time, North Vietnam began to feel the impact of the war it had launched.

"We seek no wider war," declared President Johnson, explaining the "bomb the north" campaign. But the war did widen, and there was a sense of precipitous movement towards the brink. The anxious question agitated Vietnam and the world: What will Communist China and Soviet Russia do if the attacks continue?

The North Vietnamese were unable to cope with the massive air assaults. For the most part, the South Vietnamese and American aircraft met with little resistance. Occasionally a few Russian MIGs from North Vietnamese bases endeavored to ward off the attacks, but the effect was negligible. The planes and pilots based at Da Nang, south of the 17th parallel, and the carrier-based aircraft of the American Seventh Fleet lying off the coast, were far too formidable for the limited air power at the disposal of the Hanoi regime. Almost all of North Vietnam south of the Red River became the hunting ground for American and South Vietnamese bombers. The war had definitely taken on a new look.

Sighs and growls, cheers and jeers, greeted the new turn in the Vietnam war. What did the United States hope to achieve by the counterblow against North Vietnam? Would it hasten the end of the struggle? Or was it the beginning of a Korea-type conflagration? Controversy raged all over the world.

The Saigon Government and its American advisers argued that if the North Vietnamese could cross the frontier and indulge in open aggression against the South, it was quite in order for the South Vietnamese and their allies to cross the same frontier in self-defense. They knew that Hanoi, without adequate military support from its allies in Peking and Moscow, could not long withstand the combined air power of South Vietnam, the U.S. Air Force and the Seventh Fleet. The idea was that any peace move prompted by the massive air strikes, would be advantageous to South Vietnam and help bolster the sagging anti-communist morale in Southeast Asia.

It was difficult to attempt any assessment of the popular mood in South Vietnam. Were the common people of the South opposed to the air strikes? Were they in favor of peace at any price, even surrender to communism, to avoid the consequences of a bitter aerial warfare, involving the forces of the big powers? Did they feel strongly about the bombing of the North and the toll of Vietnamese life and property resulting from it?

The consensus of opinion, at least in Siagon, seemed to favor a showdown, if it came to that, instead of the dangerous drift towards defeat and disaster. Almost everyone realized that the alternative was slavery under communist rule. Even the handful of "pacifists" who raised the vague plea for a ceasefire were not disposed to resign themselves to communist tyranny.

Talking to people in various walks of life and watching

the general reaction to the air assaults I gained the impression that the average person welcomed the new turn in the war, in spite of the dangers inherent in it. They seemed relieved that at last they were getting somewhere. There were cheers for the young airmen who took part in the raids on North Vietnam. And if there was anxiety, it was tempered with hope and the satisfaction that comes of resolute action.'

Asian nations, which had already tasted communist aggression, endorsed the American action in taking the war to communist North Vietnam. Malaysia, Thailand, the Philippines, Taiwan and South Korea welcomed it as a clear test of Communist will, as it meant a really tight squeeze not only on North Vietnam, but also on its patrons in Peking and Moscow. In Japan, the dominant theme was one of hopes for a negotiated settlement in Vietnam. India, still licking the wounds of communist Chinese aggression at the Himalayan border in 1962, joined the plea for peace and the prevention of a wider war, without directly condemning the air attacks. Several of the other non-aligned nations, including some which had often tried to toe the communist peace line, remained discreetly silent. Apparently they were happy that the communists were at last getting what they richly deserved, but felt it was safer to stick to the pious peace theme in public pronouncements.

The communist "Big Two" were aghast. In Peking, an official statement condemned the bombing attacks on North Vietnam as "undisguised war provocation" by the United States. It said: "The Democratic Republic of Vietnam is a member of the Socialist camp and all other

Socialist countries have the unshirkable international ob-
ligation to support and assist it with actual deeds . . . The
People's Republic of China and the Chinese people would
definitely not stand idly by. . . ."

Moscow was equally prompt in denouncing the American challenge. In a statement distributed by the official
Tass news agency, the Soviet Government said that it
would be forced, together with its allies and friends, to
take further measures to aid the Democratic Republic of
Vietnam, in its defense against American aggression. It
added: "The Soviet Union will definitely fulfill its international duty to the fraternal Socialist country."

The next day, North Vietnamese and Chinese communist students in Moscow staged a "spontaneous" demon-
stration at the U.S. Embassy. Communist satellites, from
Prague to Pyongyang, joined the chorus, proclaiming
their readiness to smash "U.S. imperialism."

The outlook was undoubtedly menacing. Neither Peking nor Moscow, in spite of their own feud, could allow
the satellite state of North Vietnam to be blown to bits
by American bombers. There were reports that the
Russians were sending ground-to-air missiles for the aerial
defense of Hanoi and Haiphong. Other reports claimed
that advance elements of Communist China's People's
Liberation Army had begun moving into North Vietnam.
These reports followed a statement made by Red China's
President Liu Shao Chi that any aggression against North
Vietnam was an aggression against China, strongly re-
miniscent of Peking's entry into the Korean war.

In between these dire threats and menacing gestures,
however, the communist giants taunted each other over

their Vietnam policy. China accused Russia of betraying the cause of communist North Vietnam, while Moscow claimed that Peking was deliberately obstructing the flow of Russian aid to the Hanoi regime by refusing facilities for Soviet aircraft to fly over Chinese territory.

The air raids continued without let-up. Nearly 1,800 dependents of American military and civilian personnel in South Vietnam were ordered home in what was described as a bid to "clear the decks." The British Embassy in Saigon advised British subjects in the outlying districts to move to the capital, fearing the breakdown of travel facilities. The Vietcong guerillas intensified their campaign everywhere. They blew up a section of the air base in Da Nang and, later, staged a bomb attack on the American Embassy in Saigon.

Presumably, there was some reversal of tactics by the communists. In the Gulf of Tonkin incident, in the summer of 1964, the communists tried to test the U.S. will by a PT-boat attack on units of the Seventh Fleet. They got their answer in the form of the first American air attack against North Vietnamese naval installations along the coast, but there was no immediate provocation. This time, however, after a brief re-appraisal of the situation, the communists intensified their campaign in South Vietnam and it was recognized on all sides that they were always in the advantageous position of being able to plot in secrecy, prepare in silence, and strike without forewarning precisely when and where it suited them.

·Those were hectic days in Saigon. Events were moving fast. While the air assaults continued, a major battle flared up for the control of the strategic highway linking the highlands south of the 17th parallel with the central Vietnamese coast. The communists were reported to be moving considerable forces to this vital sector in preparation for large scale mobile warfare. It was stated that about 20,000 North Vietnamese troops had crossed the demilitarized zone into South Vietnam. American and South Vietnamese air forces extended their operations to this region, where the communist forces were massing, as their movement implied a threat to the great air base in Da Nang and a bid to bring the frontier down well below the 17th parallel, with communist control over the strategic highway between the highlands and the coast.

If the Hanoi regime and its allies were unable to challenge the American-South Vietnamese air power, they concentrated their efforts on the propaganda offensive. Side by side with threats to crush U.S. "imperialism," they tried to exploit the sentiment of the people against bloodshed and destruction, without the slightest thought of their own long record of murder and arson covering all South Vietnam. Suddenly a "peace front" appeared on the horizon. Whoever conceived the idea and worked on it behind the scenes managed to secure the support of some non-partisan elements for their campaign. The plea for peace, with its magic spell on a people who had not known peace for a quarter of a century, proved a baffling challenge to the Government in Saigon, still recovering from a chain of internal upheavals.

The peace front, in a leaflet widely circulated in Saigon and elsewhere in the country, called for an immediate ceasefire, negotiations for peace with the Vietcong, and the end of all foreign intervention. The appeal had a familiar ring about it—it was precisely the pattern of communist propaganda. But the position in Saigon was that any government which opposed any move that sought peace ran the risk of being dubbed as a stooge of the Americans.

For a couple of days, neither the government nor the military junta would comment officially on the peace front and its campaign. Then cautiously the Prime Minister, Phan Huy Quat, stated that in his personal view, any peace negotiations with the communist Vietcong were not feasible at that time, while the cessation of resistance without firmly established pre-conditions would be suicidal to South Vietnam. Quietly, Quat's police picked up a few persons associated with the movement. A Buddhist leader who had earlier identified himself with the peace front backed out of it. A few others admitted they were not aware of the communist hand behind the movement. But three leaders of the campaign, a veterinary doctor, a school teacher and a journalist, were unrepentant. The Government, accusing them of communist sympathies, gave them a ceremonial send-off to communist North Vietnam at the bridge spanning the Ben Hai River that runs along the 17th parallel.

The Government's action raised another controversy. Opinion was sharply divided on the wisdom of deporting suspected pro-communists to the north and some of the newspapers asked why South Vietnam should provide useful grist to the communist propaganda mills in Hanoi and elsewhere. Anyway, the so-called peace front, which no doubt had some communist background, went into voluntary liquidation almost before it got under way.

The war was now in full swing on sea, land and in the

air. For a brief spell, the military exigency appeared to have eclipsed the perennial squabbles on Saigon's political front, forging a good measure of unity and comradeship among the leaders of the armed forces and the civilians whom they had placed in power. The reprisal raids continued, inflicting enormous damage to the Hanoi Government's war effort. Washington reiterated its stand and announced that the "key to the situation remains the cessation of infiltration from North Vietnam and the clear indication by the Hanoi regime that it is prepared to cease aggression against its neighbors."

There was no response from Hanoi, even after the U.S. Government sent out feelers that it would be prepared to suspend the bombing raids in response to some gesture from the North Vietnamese leaders. They refused to budge, stayed glum in their anger, ready for an endurance test. It seemed that their communist allies in Peking, too, were in no mood for any effective action.

To Mao Tze-tung and his henchmen in Peking, Vietnam 1965 looked entirely different from Korea 1950. The sound and fury of the Sino-Soviet alliance had died out. In its place was the bitter feud, which had transcended the levels of the ideological dialogue in which it began. The United States had warned, in unmistakable terms, that any involvement by Communist China in Vietnam would mean an open, all-out war, which Peking could not afford to risk.

The Moscow-Peking axis had been subjected to a series of violent twists. There was no certainty that the Russians would rush to the aid of China in the event of a clash of arms with the United States. On the other hand, Peking had good reason to suspect that Soviet Russia might take advantage of any misadventure in which China became involved, for a quick re-adjustment of the disputed frontiers between the two countries and the possible extension of the Soviet domain right up to the industrial heart of Manchuria. Besides, there was Generalissimo Chiang Kai-shek in Taiwan, biding his time to stage a comeback to Mainland China, and a clash between America and Peking China could well mean the realization of his dream. That was Mao's dilemma.

It was assuredly unsafe to attempt another Korea in Vietnam. The requirements of self-preservation were more pressing than loyalty for a satellite state, and far more important than a temporary loss of face within the communist bloc, with prospective allies and dupes like Indonesia's Sukarno and the communist parties in the various Southeast Asian countries. Mao, therefore, seemed inclined to consider that discretion was the better part of valor.

The propaganda factory, however, took no respite. It stepped up its output, though it offered little consolation to Ho Chi Minh and the Hanoi regime. Red China's army chief of staff, General Lo Jui-ching, denounced President Johnson as "more insidious and deadly than Hitler," condemned the Russians for their reluctance to engage in full involvement in Southeast Asia and warned "Whoever wants to satisfy his greed at the expense of others is lifting a rock that will eventually fall on his own toes."

In Saigon, as well as in Washington and many other world capitals, the new Mao line was clearly attributed to a combination of two salient factors—the inability of

Red China (and Soviet Russia) to respond adequately and the realization on their part that the risks involved were too great to justify taking a long chance.

In his cold realism, Mao decided, at least temporarily, to emulate the ancient Chinese statesman Tsao Tsao, who lived in the 3rd century A.D. and was a forerunner of today's communist leadership in establishing agro-military communes in China. Tsao Tsao's dictum was that it was better to betray others than be betrayed yourselves. And Mao Tze-tung, in his supreme wisdom, seemed to have decided that it was better to betray Ho Chi Minh than to be betrayed by his comrades in Moscow, even if it meant the ignominy of being labeled a "paper tiger."

CHAPTER 12

The American Saga

God considers not the action, but the spirit of the action. It is the intention, not the deed, wherein the merit or praise of the doer consists. Indeed, the same action is done from different motives: for the sake of justice by one man, for an evil reason by another.

Peter Abelard

·AN INCREDIBLY strange feature of the war in Vietnam is the deep, almost irrevocable, involvement of the United States in it.·The U.S. commitment in this war of resistance against aggression in South Vietnam is so heavy that the new phase of the conflict has come to be regarded as an American war.

·Eleven years ago, before Dien Bien Phu and the Geneva agreements, the United States evinced scant interest in Vietnam: Had America desired to prop up French colonialism, or seek a share in the spoils of the colonial war, the months before Dien Bien Phu were ideal to pursue those objectives. But the Washington Administration stayed aloof. The French were forced out of Indochina and

General de Gaulle, with his new-found neutralist cure for Vietnam, must be rubbing his hands in glee at the way the United States has become bogged down in the Vietnamese quagmire.

American sacrifices in the U.N. war of resistance against communist aggression in Korea were enormous. The lessons of that conflict were inescapable. No nation would be secure, no frontier would be safe, if the neighbor happened to be communist. Besides, the human problem of dealing with the flood of refugees from communist terror and tyranny was just as vital as the military operations to ward off communist aggression.

The advent of a communist regime in North Vietnam was the signal for a heavy influx of refugees to South Vietnam. Those days, the people had the choice between the communist north and the non-communist south. More than a million Vietnamese moved to the south, while less than ten percent of that number opted for the Hanoi regime. And, when the late Ngo Dinh Diem sought American assistance for the transport of these refugees and their re-settlement in the South, the United States helped the Saigon Government in a big way. American transport ships ferried the refugees from Haiphong to Saigon, and the U.S. Government and a number of U.S. agencies helped finance their rehabilitation in new surroundings.

What began as a purely humanitarian endeavor has now brought the United States to the brink of a major war in Southeast Asia. That is the irony of the American involvement in Vietnam.

In October, 1954, when President Eisenhower made the first official announcement of U.S. readiness to help

South Vietnam develop "a strong and viable state, capable of resisting attempted subversion or aggression," what the Washington Administration offered was a mere token of goodwill and support—financial assistance to the tune of U.S. $300,000,000 a year and about 500 military advisers. By May, 1965, U.S. military combat strength in South Vietnam rose to nearly 60,000 and more battalions of marines and navy seabees were on the way. Total U.S. costs in Vietnam rose to almost $1,000,000,000 a year.

The big jump in military and economic assistance began in 1961, following the upsurge of Vietcong terror and subversion, when it was established that the guerillas were directed and controlled by the Hanoi government. President Kennedy, in a policy statement, affirmed that the U.S. was "determined Vietnam shall not be lost to the communists for lack of any support which the U.S. Government can render." The communists took the cue and revised their strategy and tactics accordingly.

The American assistance program has expanded steadily since then. U.S. military personnel grew in number, almost every month. They were no longer simple advisers. They figured in combat actions. They piloted helicopters carrying Vietnamese troops. They helped the defense of strategic villages in the countryside. By mid-June 1965, more than five hundred had been killed in attacks by, or in action against, the communist invaders, in addition to many more hundreds wounded in combat actions and Vietcong terrorist outrages.

The Vietcong forces and their patrons in Hanoi and Peking kept up the offensive. In March 1964, U.S. Defense Secretary McNamara reported that the situation in South Vietnam had "unquestionably worsened" and that the communist conquest of South Vietnam would result in the conquest of all Southeast Asia by the Chinese communists. He said the Washington Administration was diametrically opposed to "suggestions of withdrawal or neutralization" in Vietnam's war of resistance against communist aggression. Four months later, he told the American Senate's Foreign Relations Committee that the U.S. efforts in South Vietnam carried "the risk of escalating to military actions outside the border of South Vietnam." The forecast came true in February, 1965, with the air strikes across the 17th parallel.

After a hundred days of bombing attacks on targets in North Vietnam, President Johnson made this clarification of the aims and objectives of the United States: "We know, as our adversaries should also know, that there is no purely military solution in sight for either side. We are ready for unconditional discussions. Most of the non-communist nations of the world favor such unconditional discussions. And it would clearly be in the interests of North Vietnam to now come to the conference table. For them, the continuation of war without talks means only damage without conquest."

The President also served a virtual ultimatum on Communist China. He said: "Communist China apparently desires the war to continue. Their target is not merely South Vietnam. It is Asia. Their objective is not the fulfillment of Vietnamese nationalism. It is to erode and to discredit America's ability to help prevent Communist China's domination over all of Asia. In this domination, they shall never succeed."

That was the mark of the United States involvement in Vietnam and its will to assist the "stop the reds" campaign in Southeast Asia. President Johnson went on record with these and a series of equally emphatic statements, affirming American policy in unmistakable terms, while a major controversy raged across the country over America's role in Vietnam. It was a dialog between some of the learned pundits of American journalism and the academic world.

SAMPLE VIEWS:

Hans J. Morgenthau, *Professor of Political Science at the University of Chicago:* "We must learn to accommodate ourselves to the predominance of China on the Asian mainland. It is instructive to note that those Asian nations which have done so—such as Burma and Cambodia— live peacefully in the shadow of the Chinese giant . . . Ho Chi Minh will become the leader of a Chinese satellite only if the United States forces him to become one. . . ."

Columnist Joseph Alsop: "Professor Morgenthau is an interesting figure; for he plays almost the same key role among the modern appeasers that Geoffrey Dawson of *The Times* (London) played in the be-nice-to-Hitler group in England before 1939 . . . One way to solve the problem *(of Vietnam and Asia)* is to recognize the Chinese communists as the Asian Herrenvolk and to allow them to gobble their neighbors at will, even if their neighbors happen to be our allies and friends. If Morgenthau possessed enough forthrightness to recommend this solution, he could not be called ignorant, although he might perhaps be criticized on other grounds."

Columnist Walter Lippman: "Why is it, it is time

to ask, that our position in Asia has declined so sharply, though we are widening and intensifying the war in Vietnam? Today, the United States is not only isolated but increasingly opposed by every major power in Asia. The Administration must put this fact in its pipe and smoke it. It should ponder the fact that there exists such general Asian opposition to our war in Asia . . . We shall find ourselves widely rejected by the very people we are professing to save . . ."

Columnist Max Lerner (listing the arguments and the answers): *That the Vietnam war is not the result of communist aggression but is a spontaneous uprising of the Viet people to decide their own destiny.*

The Vietcong (Viet Communists) have exploited, led, organized, sustained and (since 1961) completely taken over the movement, with training, supplies and support from Hanoi.

That the U.S. is practicing imperialism and committing atrocities in the war.

If "imperialism" means the use of massive power, then yes, but that is a meaningless meaning, since fighting always means the use of power.

That America cannot find or maintain a stable government in South Vietnam.

There was such a government under Diem; there can be a better one when the fighting stops. Communism is a one-way street. Non-communist regimes can be changed, improved, as the examples of Brazil, Peru, Chile show.

It is only a mature democracy that can thrive on public controversies such as this. That is not to suggest that the communist countries do not have people with ideas and opinion. But they are gagged by a regime that does all the thinking and talking for all the people.

In South Vietnam, in spite of the curbs on freedom of the press, you still come across scores of people who talk freely and frankly, and sometimes vehemently, against the policies of their government, against the attitude of American aid officials and advisers working in the country. In Japan, there have been "Yankee, Go Home!" demonstrations. In South Vietnam, there have been demands for the "end of all foreign intervention." Neither of these moves, however, represented any significant section of public opinion. And, if we have not heard of any North Vietnamese protest against their government's suicidal policy, it is just because the Hanoi regime is a police state.

An alien armed force is unpopular in any country. The prejudice is particularly deep in the newly-independent Asian countries, where misunderstandings arise even when foreign military personnel are there as allies at the invitation of the governments concerned. When there is an insidious campaign against those allies by elements operating against them, within the country, the difficulties of understanding and adjustment become highly magnified. Considering these basic factors, the American military advisory group and combatant forces are more than welcome in Vietnam and among the Vietnamese officials, armed forces personnel and the people. They know that the Americans are bearing the brunt of the battle, in which the stakes are high—the freedom and independence of their country.

Foreign bases and foreign military personnel do not add to the prestige of a free nation, though such great powers as Britain, Japan and Germany seem to recognize that they can be an asset to national security and defense preparedness in the context of present-day strategic requirements.

Communist China received considerable military assistance from the Soviet Union. Thousands of Russian advisers and experts served in Red China until a couple of years ago, before the ideological dispute resulted in the withdrawal of the once-favored "dabizu" (big nose) allies. Japan, Nationalist China, the Republic of Korea, the Philippines and Malaysia have foreign bases and foreign military personnel under freely negotiated mutual defense arrangements which have not in any way disparaged their status as independent nations.

North Korea and North Vietnam are virtually protectorates of Communist China, while many of the other nations of Asia know that their independence and neutrality remain unimpaired only at the pleasure of the communist giant across the frontier.

Some of the so-called non-aligned nations, taking advantage of their geographic location, have strengthened themselves militarily with arms and equipment, naval craft and air force planes, acquired on credit and through false promises, from rival power blocs in the global cold war, only to use them for local conquests. This is precisely what Indonesia has done.

Neutrality and non-alignment, based on an idealistic concept of international relations, like the policy advocated by the late Jawaharlal Nehru, and by Thailand before World War II, not only failed to discourage external aggression, but even served as an invitation to aggression by unscrupulous conquerors.

If truth is the first causualty of war, the independence and neutrality of the militarily weak nations lead the list of targets in expansionist plots, always and everywhere. That explains the fighting in Laos, the plight of Burma and Cambodia, the spate of communist infiltration and subversion in the Himalayan region and all along the northern borders of the Middle Eastern nations, and the Peking regime's military aggression against India. The remedy lies in all aggressors and potential aggressors renouncing expansionism and conquest, not only by force of arms, but also through the more insidious tactics such as subversion and terror.

When President Sukarno of Indonesia, waging his confrontation campaign against Malaysia, insists that the British bases and military units be withdrawn from that country, his objective is to gobble up Malaysia without serious effort. Similarly, when communist North Vietnam and the Peking regime in China denounce the United States as an "imperialist aggressor" in Vietnam, it is for the simple reason that the Americans are making it difficult for them to take over South Vietnam and extend the communist conquest to all Southeast Asia. They seem to have immense faith in the theory that a true but complicated idea has always less chance of succeeding than one which is false but simple.

The average Asian is extremely proud and sensitive. After decades of colonial domination, he hates to bow his head to anyone, even his friends and allies, if they demand such obeisance as a matter of right, in return for help rendered. But the same pride makes him suspicious of the high-sounding slogans and sweet-smelling pledges of the new crop of sawdust Caesars in his midst in the post-independence era.

The role of the United States in South Vietnam is, in many respects, similar to that of Britain in Malaysia, though the circumstances of the involvement and the operational environment are different. Another major difference is that the war in Vietnam has been longer, more fierce, and fraught with more dangerous potentialities than Sukarno's "on again, off again" armed action against Malaysia. Both, however, are cases of deliberate external aggression. And history is full of instances in which victims of aggression have sought, and obtained, the assistance of friends and allies in the struggle for national survival.

If the war in Vietnam is the product of communist aggression, organized, directed and controlled by the Lao Dong Party which operates from Hanoi, the anti-Malyasia confrontation is instigated and supported by the Communist Party of Indonesia which is in a position to dictate the policy of the Sukarno regime. There may be some sort of vague co-ordination between these two conflicts in Southeast Asia. Perhaps the high priests of Asian communism in Peking are plotting further actions on the same pattern elsewhere. But for the time being, there is little doubt that Hanoi and Peking are out on a war of conquest. And the question is whether other nations of the world have a right, and a duty, to help the victims of aggression.

There can be no two answers to this question. And

yet, we are in the midst of a raging, tearing controversy over the role of the United States in Vietnam.

Why? Because, as T.S. Eliot puts it in his inimitable way "Few now claim the free speech to call a knave a knave, or a fool a fool."

CHAPTER 13

"Riding the Tiger"

A 250,000-man French expeditionary force came this way and was destroyed. Don't let it happen to you.
    Vietcong signboard on South Vietnam highway.

FOUR MONTHS of almost incessant air assaults on North Vietnamese military targets, and at least three peace plans and offers of negotiations, produced no response from Hanoi or Peking. The bomb strikes certainly hurt the Hanoi regime and its war effort. They revived the squabble within North Vietnam's ruling Politburo, sharply divided between the Moscow and Peking lines. But the ominous silence continued, amidst fresh reports that Communist China had started a vast movement of troops, rockets, guns and ammunition to the Vietnamese border.

Meanwhile, there was no let-up in the Vietcong activity. In many areas they began massing in larger numbers than ever before. On the highway south of the American base in Da Nang, where big concentrations of Vietcong troops were reported, they put up a signboard warning the American and South Vietnamese forces against a disaster of the Dien Bien Phu type, which befell the French colonial forces in 1954. It seemed fairly certain that the Vietcong was preparing for a big assault somewhere, hoping to inflict a crushing defeat on the South Vietnamese and American forces, as a preface to any negotiations which, they hope, will put them inside the Government in some capacity. From that to complete take-over should be a comparatively easy move.

The American air strikes were launched with the object of warning the Hanoi regime and crippling the flow of troops and war material from North Vietnam to the South. But it looked as if the war in South Vietnam would continue, even if the bombing raids were extended to the Hanoi and Haiphong regions. The orthodox American answer to the unorthodox threats of the communists in Vietnam had apparently produced only limited results. The communists believe in the dictum that you cannot exterminate a swarm of ants with an iron pickhead.

The debate was on again. How effective was air strength, against an elusive guerilla movement that merged with the countryside and the masses of the people at the first sign of trouble? Were all the bomb strikes on North Vietnam going to prove a costly and futile effort? These and other questions intrigued and agitated policymakers and strategists alike. But neither could hazard a convincing answer.

In many engagements in the Vietnamese countryside, massive air support has contributed to the victory of the Vietnamese security forces. Transport of troops by helicopters has often helped the government forces in crucial battles. Close-support aircraft, armed helicopters and artillery have been of considerable assistance in the anti-Vietcong operations. Yet the war on the ground knows no respite, and the Vietcong seem stronger and more active than ever before.

. In spite of all the U.S. assistance in men and money, aircraft and modern weapons, the areas under the Saigon Government's control have become progressively smaller. The communists have undermined the authority of the government by the selective assassination of civil servants and village headmen, by systematic terror and kidnap campaigns, through tactics of persuasion and propaganda. Naturally, the communists were not inclined to rush to the negotiating table, until the air strikes on North Vietnam aroused second thoughts in their minds.`

North Vietnamese leaders, inclined to toe the Moscow line, were reported to be aiming at a big military push, to be followed by negotiations which would mean the consolidation of communist gains but a postponement of the take-over of South Vietnam. Premier Pham Van Dong and the Army Chief, General Vo Nguyen Giap, were understood to favor this plan of action, while other members of the Politburo, led by the Assembly Chairman Truong Trinh (Long March) were known to be insisting on the hard line set by Peking. Their demands included the withdrawal of U.S. troops before agreeing to negotiations. They know there need be no negotiations at all, after the withdrawal of American forces from South Vietnam.

President Ho Chi Minh, caught between the rival factions, favors the Russian brand of communism and a line of action acceptable to the comrades in Moscow. But he cannot ignore the dictates of the Chinese communist leadership, just across the frontier. The time for decision may come with the extension of the bomb strikes to Hanoi. In mid-May, 1965, the Hanoi authorities began moving the important government departments from the city to the countryside. They also ordered dependents of officials to evacuate the capital. In a strange, inexplicable way, Hanoi seemed prepared for anything—even national suicide.

If Hanoi was in jitters, Saigon, too, had a fair share of the usual troubles during May, just when the war hit the decisive phase. After three months of comparative stability, the Government headed by Premier Phan Huy Quat seemed well settled in the saddle of political power. The powerful Armed Forces Council had dissolved itself, reflecting the Generals' confidence in the civilian cabinet. Then, suddenly, Saigon was in the midst of another coup—this time a coup inspired, at least partly, by the communist Vietcong. The Government announced that the coup had been foiled and the storm blew over soon with the arrest of a few army officers and a minor re-organization of the cabinet. The significant fact, however, was that if the coup had proved successful, it could have paved the way for an eventual communist take-over in South Vietnam.

Presumably, the Vietcong had been infiltrating into the armed forces of South Vietnam, sowing the seeds of disaffection among the junior officers and perhaps even some of the senior military leaders, taking advantage of the unending rivalry and struggle for power between them.

In spite of the mystery that shrouded the origin of the plot and the way it was dealt with by the Saigon Government and the leaders of the armed forces, there was little doubt that communist subversion had been extended to cover at least some elements in the defense services.

The situation became increasingly precarious. Every party involved in the Vietnam war was caught on the horns of a dilemma-each of the available alternatives was equally undesirable. The war dragged on, with no end in sight, in spite of the recognition on all sides that it could well end in an appalling international collision.

The American air strikes continued. There was no desire to indulge in destructive bombing on a large scale, because the original objective was only to bring the North Vietnamese to the conference table. Yet the raids were pursued with increased intensity, as the Hanoi regime ignored the offers of a negotiated settlement.

•Public opinion in the United States was stirred by the latest trend of the war in Vietnam. Waging a costly war, with increased American involvement in Vietnam and Southeast Asia, was not precisely the Washington Administration's basic purpose. But there was no way out. The commitments were grave and any withdrawal from Vietnam was unthinkable.•

In many of the languages of the Orient, they have a picturesque way of describing the plight in which the United States finds itself in Vietnam. They call it "riding the tiger." It is an awful ordeal for the rider but he just could not think of dismounting, as he would be an easy prey for the tiger.

In the strange mess that is Vietnam today, the misfortune of "riding the tiger" is spread all round. Nobody is spared; the dilemma is common to all.

Vietcong casualties have been heavy since the beginning of 1965. For a brief spell the Vietcong seemed disposed to lie low, but that meant death or capture, and their leaders in far-away Hanoi and Peking wanted the war to be stepped up. So, they go on fighting—and dying. They just cannot think of surrender, except on rare occasions when they are singularly fortunate, as they would be shot down by the hard-core fanatics among their own comrades. The Vietcong guerillas and their leaders are in a fix, in spite of their propagandist threats. In a way, they too are "riding the tiger."

There is no doubt that the leaders in Hanoi are in the same plight. They cannot be enjoying the grim spectacle of their country going up in flames, their factories and military installations being smashed by American bombs. They cannot risk discontent and revolt by the people, in spite of the vast powers they wield over them. But they are not free agents. They have to consider the Peking tiger which has taken them on a joy ride. In the mystic ways of Mao-ism, there is no guarantee that a paper tiger cannot suddenly turn into a killer on the prowl.

The Peking Tiger itself is in no better plight. It is riding a tiger of its own creation. It was Communist China that sponsored and directed the "war of liberation" in South Vietnam, through its agents and associates in Hanoi. The objective was to extend communist conquest to all Southeast Asia after the take-over in South Vietnam. But the campaign has not worked out according to plans because the Americans have come to the rescue of South Vietnam.

Mao Tze-tung wants the Vietnam war to continue. He is out to resist so-called U.S. imperialism—to the last Vietnamese. Much as Mao would perhaps like to intervene in Vietnam, with his enormous manpower, just as he did in Korea, he finds his allies in Moscow thoroughly undependable and his adversaries in Washington prepared to risk a major war, if necessary. And he is not prepared for the risk which might prove suicidal to the Peking regime.

Mao is in no happy position. He, too, rides the tiger, weary and reluctant, hoping for a miracle which will save Vietnam for communism—and save his own face into the bargain.

The sphinx in Peking, like all others involved in the Vietnamese mess, may be on the horns of a major dilemma, but it still dominates the Southeast Asian horizon, with the irresistible question: What's Mao up to?

The question loomed larger and more urgent after Communist China exploded yet another nuclear bomb in May.

Is Mao massing his troops for a showdown in Vietnam?

Is he so frustrated with the ordeal of riding the tiger that he is seriously thinking of dismounting—with all the fateful consequences?

CHAPTER 14

Towards Showdown?

I sit on a man's back, choking him and making him carry me, and yet I assure myself and others that I am very sorry for him and wish to ease his lot by all possible means—except by getting off his back.

Tolstoy

THE CLOUDS hung low over the Vietnamese sky—thick, dark and menacing. And, then the rains came—brief, light showers at first, followed by a heavy, incessant downpour. Rivers, streams and canals rose swiftly. Miles and miles of paddy fields were flooded. The fury of the monsoon covered all Southeast Asia. There was stagnation all round, except on the bitter fighting fronts in the Vietnamese countryside and the turbulent political front in Saigon.

June dawned bleak on war-weary Vietnam. The air raids on military targets in North Vietnam continued without let-up. The Vietnamese military leaders and their American allies made feverish preparations to cope with the monsoon offensive expected to be launched by the Vietcong forces. But the element of surprise rested, as always, with the Vietcong. And as the rains pelted down, hampering the movement of heavy vehicles on the roads and the deployment of air power, the communist invaders from the north moved out in strength from their hideouts, smashing at government posts with devastating effect.

This time, it was a new type of war which the Vietcong launched in various sectors. The attacks were made by the hard core of communist forces. Their firepower was formidable, with bazookas, heavy mortars, machine guns and artillery. It seemed that the Vietcong had cast aside the thin disguise in which they had been operating hitherto. This was open warfare, with the Vietcong throwing thousands of men into battle, in a desperate bid to gain the initiative they had lost, at any sacrifice in men and material. More fully equipped combat units had crossed the border into South Vietnam for the momentous monsoon offensive.

The Vietcong objective was the provincial capital of Quang Ngai, in the central Vietnam highlands. They launched a massive attack west of the town, wiping out an entire government unit. The Government forces mounted a counter-attack and forced the Vietcong to pull back, after a pitched battle. The Government losses were heavy but the Vietcong casualties were heavier. The town of Quang Ngai was saved and the Vietcong plans to set up a provisional government in South Vietnam were foiled.

But the monsoon offensive had only begun. In spite of the Quang Ngai disaster, the Vietcong launched a series of ambushes in the nearby provinces of Darlac, Pleiku and Phu Bon, inflicting enormous losses on the government forces. Side by side, the communists stepped up the tempo of their campaign of sabotage, murder and destruction. Despite the adverse weather, though, the air forces continued to operate, with devastating effect on Vietcong morale. An announcement in Washington said that General William C. Westmoreland, Commander of the U.S. Military Assistance Command, had been empowered to commit U.S. troops in support of South Vietnamese forces, if the necessity arose.

The Vietcong, racing against time to score a decisive victory before the end of the monsoon season, disregarded the threat and the prospect of further defeat and disaster. Their next big target was another district capital, Dong Xoai, about 55 miles north of Saigon. In a surprise night attack, the Vietcong shock troops were all over the place, mowing down the defenders and slaughtering the townspeople. In a few hours, South Vietnamese and American aircraft appeared over the embattled town and relief forces arrived by helicopter. According to eye-witnesses, the battle for Dong Xoai was probably the bloodiest military action in Indochina since Dien Bien Phu. But unlike Dien Bien Phu, when it ended the communists were routed in disorder, leaving behind more than 700 dead. The defenders' toll was also considerable—about 200 dead and scores wounded.

The battles raged, loud and long, all over South Vietnam. It was evident, however, that the communists were not having their way. The Peking regime renewed its threat to send its " volunteers " into the Vietnam war— if requested by Hanoi to do so. It claimed that the United States Government's decision to order its troops to take an active part in the war in Vietnam was "an adventurous act which will bring about great consequences." There were further reports of Chinese troop concentrations at the frontier with North Vietnam and "war-like" preparedness along the Chinese coastline. Other reports said that Soviet Russia was expediting large scale military assistance to North Vietnam, during the crucial phase of the war.

All indications, however, were that both Peking and Moscow were awaiting the outcome of the monsoon offensive for any move they might make. Neither Moscow nor Peking seemed eager to take the plunge and precipitate a Korea-type war in Vietnam. They waited on the sidelines, cheering the Hanoi regime, while its soliders died by the hundreds every day on the hills and plains of South Vietnam in a bitter, all-out battle in the cause of communist expansionism.

Like Tolstoy's man on the other man's back, they would not get off Hanoi's back; nor would they let Comrade Ho get off the back of South Vietnam. That was the mark of communist solidarity, as the Vietcong's monsoon offensive got under way in the Vietnam war!

Yet, they were adamant in their campaign of aggression. They spurned peace moves, emanating from all directions. President Johnson's offer of peace talks without pre-conditions was rejected outright, even after the United States tacitly suspended the air attacks on North Vietnam. The common stand, agreed upon by Hanoi, Peking and Moscow, was that the United States forces must withdraw from South Vietnam before any peace negotiations, the implication being that there would be no settlement other than the communist conquest of South Vietnam and its acceptance by the world.

Communist expansionism knows no compromise. It is not prepared to grant that the Republic of Vietnam has the right of freedom from attack. The Peking-Moscow-Hanoi reaction to the Commonwealth Prime Ministers' proposal of a peace mission offers eloquent proof of the communist thinking on how they wish, and hope, to end the war in Vietnam.

It is this attitude, assumed by the self-confessed agressors, that has strengthened the position of South Vietnam, in spite of its inherent weakness in the military and political spheres. South Vietnam, its government and people, merely want to be left alone, to be free from aggression from the outside. The United States, assisting South Vietnam in its defense against aggression, does not want an expansion of the war. It is ready to withdraw its forces from the country as soon as aggression ceases, and it is prepared for unconditional discussions to end the hostilities. But the communists have entirely different ideas on ending the war in Vietnam.

Many nations have, therefore, come to the assistance of the Republic of Vietnam. Countries sending aid include Australia, New Zealand, Korea, Belgium, Brazil, Canada, Austria, Denmark, Germany, Italy, Japan, Malaysia, the Netherlands, Sweden, Switzerland, the Philippines and the United Kingdom. Some have sent military and technical personnel, while others have contributed equipment, medical and other aid.

The trends are unmistakable. If the Hanoi regime's

patrons in Peking and Moscow decide on intervention in Vietnam, they may well expect another Korea-type war, if not an even bigger conflagration. Apparently, neither Peking nor Moscow is ready for it, because they know that even the non-aligned nations, which abhor war as zealously as they cherish their independence, will extend their moral support to any campaign aimed at checking aggression, in their own long-range interest.

Vietnamese politicians and military leaders realize that the war they are waging cannot be won by military might alone—that it is as much a war to crush the communist Vietcong aggressors as it is a war to win the hearts and minds of the people south of the partition line and, eventually, to win over the people across the 17th parallel. They know that, more than the guns, helicopters and artillery, it is the psychological weapons that will bring them ultimate victory. It is this weapon that the Vietcong have been exploiting effectively and indiscriminately. And it is this weapon that has been in short supply in the armory of the South Vietnamese leadership.

As the monsoon gathered momentum, the military situation began to stabilize. It would be a season of heavy fighting, with the Vietcong going all-out for a significant victory, which would place them in a position of advantage at any peace negotiations to be agreed upon at a later stage. It meant fateful days ahead for the Vietnamese people, with all the attendant suffering and privation. But the outlook in general was not desperate, especially as the United States made it abundantly clear that it was definitely committed to prevent a communist victory in Vietnam.

That seemed to settle the military issue but the political front in Saigon remained as unsettled as ever, even as the communist Vietcong forces were slaughtering the South Vietnamese troops in some of the most crucial battles of the war. Amidst reports of valor and heroism from the far-flung battle fronts, Saigon echoed with the rumblings of another political crisis and another change of government.

When Prime Minister Phan Huy Quat reluctantly assumed office in mid-February, Saigon's political seismologists gave him a month. Dr. Quat, however, disappointed the prophets, won the confidence of the Armed Forces Council, tried his best to streamline the administration, and toured the country several times in a determined bid to bolster the morale of the people and step up the anti-communist war effort. Yet less than four months after taking over the reins of government, Quat and his cabinet were swept away in Saigon's interminable political intrigues and religious squabbles.

Dr. Quat was Lieutenant-General Khanh's choice—and Khanh made the choice with the approval of the Buddhist leaders, whose campaign had resulted in the dismissal of his predecessor, Tran Van Houng. Quite naturally, Quat was what the non-Buddhist sections of the Vietnamese people called pro-Buddhist, though his record in office did not reveal any significant tendencies of religious or sectarian favoritism. But the influential Catholic section of the politically over-conscious Saigon population started getting restive, organized rallies and demonstrations and demanded the resignation of the Quat government.

Complicating the situation was Premier Quat's personal squabble with the Chief of State, Phan Khac Suu, who insisted on exercising his prerogatives to veto the Premier's proposals for the reorganization of the cabinet. The crisis deepened soon and the government machinery was almost paralyzed.

The Generals, busy with the new phase of the Vietcong campaign and reluctant to get involved in politics, were highly embarrassed. Quat tried in vain to arrive at a compromise with the Chief of State and the Catholic agitators. Finally, in despair, he informed the Generals that he wished to resign and turn over to the military the "responsibility" of leading the nation.

He was Vietnam's seventh premier to fall in 19 months of the most crucial phase of the war. And it was abundantly evident that there was no hope of establishing a stable civilian government in Saigon until after the end of the war.

It was a hard decision for the military leaders to take. There were ambitious men among them and it was difficult to evolve a formula to deal with the political crisis. They had to take over the responsibility of government but they were not sure whether they should put power in the hands of a single strong man, a military junta, or a combined military-civilian council. An almost endless series of conferences took place in Saigon, while tension ran high in the city and rumor-mongers busied themselves with talks of a major split among the Generals. Finally, though, the crisis was resolved, as were other crises before it.

Civilian Chief of State Phan Khac Suu and Prime Minister Phan Huy Quat were out. Representatives of the armed forces assumed both positions. South Vietnam settled down to yet another experiment in evolving political stability in a land that has known nothing but discord and strife, distress and bloodshed, for the best part of a quarter-century.

Viewed against the background of Vietnamese coups and countercoups, and the series of political changes and the way they have taken place, the exit of Suu and Quat was inevitable. Suu had weathered many a storm in which, like the proverbial bamboo, he swayed every time in the direction of the prevailing political wind and survived its impact. Dr. Quat established his statesmanship by the simple record of staying in office for nearly four months, much longer than the average span of premiership in the post-Diem era in Vietnam.

As politicians and public men, without popular backing, both Suu and Quat were swept away by war-time Vietnam's turbulent political tide. In spite of their political maturity and experience, neither of them was endowed with the ability to impose himself on the Vietnamese people, in their hour of crisis, by sheer force of personality, and to develop some common Vietnamese denomination to rally the nation to war and victory.

The new leadership does not look very impressive, but it may succeed where others before it have failed. 42-year-old Major General Nguyen Van Thieu is a veteran soldier, former Vice Premier and Defense Minister, older than the group of Vietnamese generals known as the " Young Turks." Besides, he is regarded as a skillful diplomat and tactful mediator. He commands the loyalty of the younger generals and the respect of the various political factions and religious sects. As Chairman of the military junta, and as Chief of State in the midst of a raging, tearing war all over the country, General Thieu has a formidable task. But there are few men in Vietnam today, who can match his ability and devotion to duty.

Air Vice-Marshal Nguyen Cao Ky, who heads the new Government of Vietnam, is one of the most colorful figures among the "Young Turks" of the Vietnamese armed forces. This dashing young airman, who has just turned 34, led the resistance against the anti-Khanh coup d'etat in February—and, then the coup which ousted Khanh himself. He combines glamor and dynamism with the capacity for hard work and daring action. Often he has led the Vietnamese air force units in raids on North Vietnam military targets. After the exile of Khanh, Ky set himself up as a coup-breaker and he may therefore be depended upon to be skillful in preventing possible coups against himself.

Nguyen Cao Ky, however, is a controversial figure. Vietnamese politicians consider him as a dangerous hothead. Some of the other " Young Turks " in the army think he is far too ambitious. In recent months, though, the young airman has shown increasing maturity and stability, and capacity for determined leadership.

Perhaps Vietnam, after years of trial and error, conflict and frustration, has at last found the right leadership. Who knows whether coup-breaker Ky (pronounced 'key') may not produce the key to Vietnamese unity—and victory in the struggle for survival?

Epilogue

THE GRIM conflict grinds on across the tortured land. Hundreds of young men die on the battlefields every day. Hundreds more are wounded and maimed. And thousands of innocent men, women and children are rendered destitute in the fierce orgy of blood, sweat and tears.

The struggle in Vietnam is no civil war. It is more than a war between North and South Vietnam. Vietnam presents the tragic spectacle of a nation, partitioned between two ideologies, caught in the vortex of the global cold war and going to pieces in the process. Ho Chi Minh's bid to conquer South Vietnam has developed into a struggle between the big power blocs, a tussle between the indomitable and the irresistible, with absolutely unpredictable possibilities.

It is certainly possible to negotiate a truly just and honorable peace in Vietnam. As in Korea fifteen years ago, so in Vietnam, it was the communists who started the war and it can end only when they cease their aggression. Any other settlement will be a travesty of justice and a betrayal of the cause of human freedom.

Peace, like mercy, is twice blest. It blesseth him that

gives and him that takes. But it is futile to expect the blessings of peace from the aggressor. The only way to peace with freedom and honor, is to convince the aggressor that aggression will not pay. But the snag is that he does not reach that conviction easily, and through entirely peaceful means.

And so we have wars, unwanted and ruinous as they are, to resist the war-makers, who believe in force and will not bow before anything else. Like the war against Hitler and the war in Korea, the war in Vietnam can only end with the retreat of the aggressor. Any other outcome will mean the enslavement of not only Vietnam, but all Southeast Asia. And the process of communist conquest may not end there.

Today, the outlook is bleak. Treachery and violence fill the air. The din of battle rises far above the fury of the monsoon storms. It is frightening to consider the consequences, in terms of human life and limb, and the moral degeneration of mankind, if the big powers turn Vietnam into a testing ground for their deadly weapons of destruction.

In the context of current realities, however, there is little likelihood of any further escalation of the Vietnam war. The ugly situation now prevailing may endure for some time, at a high pitch of tension, and perhaps heavier toll of human life, during the crucial months ahead.

The forces of peace have an uncanny knack of over-reaching the forces of war. It is a question of time and environment. The war in Vietnam must end one way or the other, at a conference table somewhere, some time. Perhaps the manner in which the hostilities cease will be not only a detente, but also some sort of rapprochement among all the parties concerned.

Soon, the roar of thunder will cease, like the guns that will be silenced. Flashes of lightning, like the flares to track down the lurking enemy, will no more stab the placid sky. The menacing clouds will melt away, like a spent force in disorderly retreat. And the cool dawn of peace will smile again on the ever-green countryside in all its fragrance and glory.